Kyle of Lochalsh

WALKS

Compiled by
Terry Marsh

Text: Terry Marsh
Photography: Terry Marsh
Editors: Crawford Gillan, Sonya Calton
Designer: Doug Whitworth

Series Consultant: Brian Conduit

Jarrold Publishing ISBN 0-7117-2419-9

While every care has been taken to ensure the accuracy of the route directions, the publishers cannot accept responsibility for errors or omissions, or for changes in details given. The countryside is not static: hedges and fences can be removed, field boundaries can be altered, footpaths can be rerouted and changes in ownership can result in the closure or diversion of some concessionary paths. Also, paths that are easy and pleasant for walking in fine conditions may become slippery, muddy and difficult in wet weather, while stepping-stones across rivers and streams may become impassable.

If you find an inaccuracy in either the text or maps, please write or e-mail to Jarrold Publishing at the addresses below.

First published 2003
by Jarrold Publishing

Printed in Belgium
by Proost NV, Turnhout. 1/03

Jarrold Publishing
Pathfinder Guides, Whitefriars, Norwich NR3 1TR
E-mail: info@totalwalking.co.uk
www. totalwalking.co.uk

Front cover: The bay at Arcairseid an Rubha and Kyle of Lochalsh (inset)
Previous page: View of the Cuillin from Arcairseid an Rubha

Contents

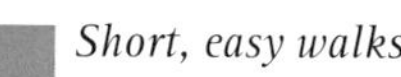
Short, easy walks

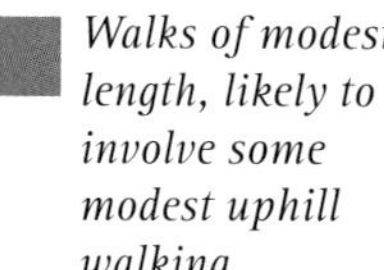
Walks of modest length, likely to involve some modest uphill walking

More challenging walks which may be longer and/or over more rugged terrain, often with some stiff climbs

Keymap

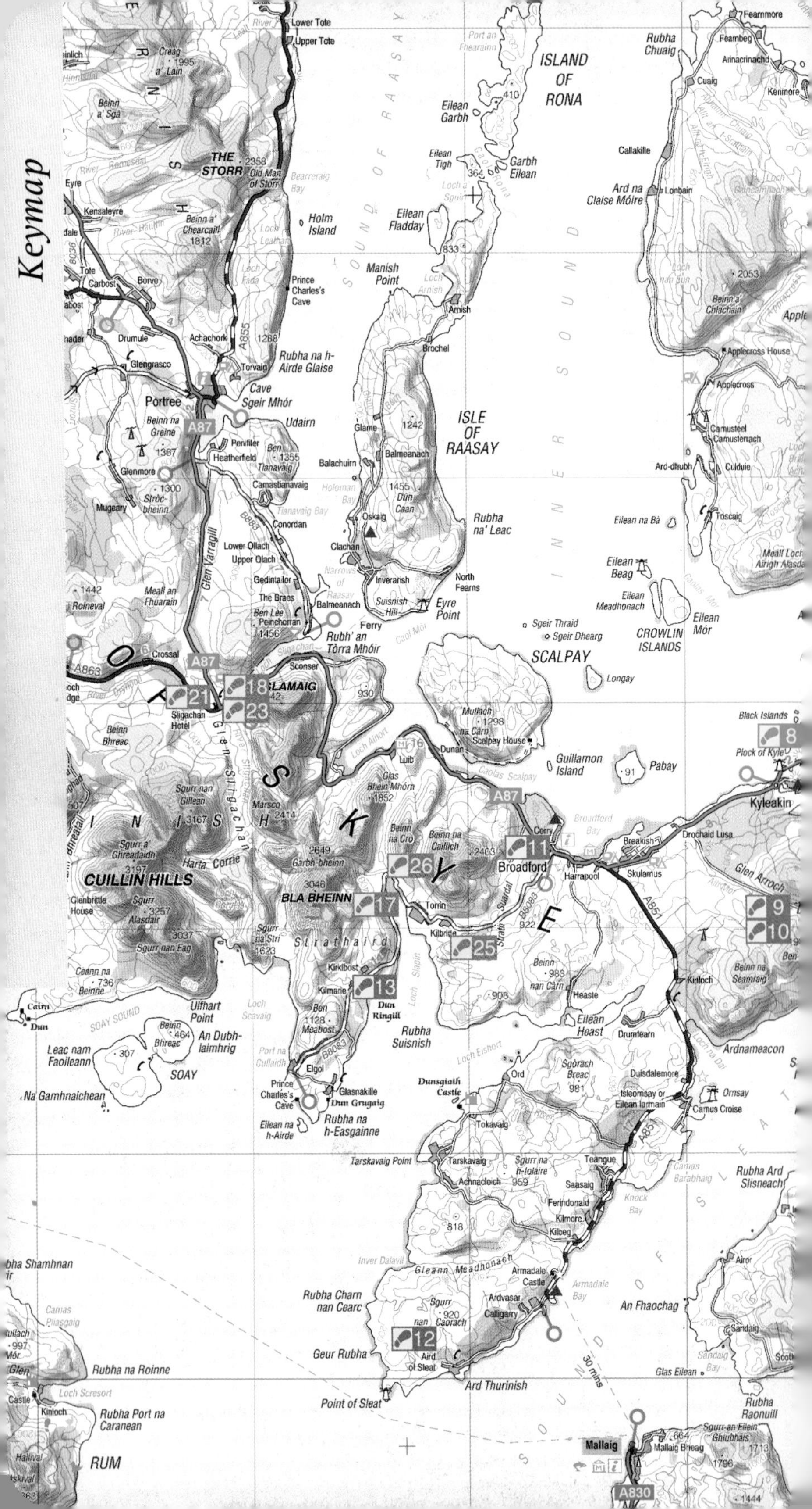

Lower Tote
Upper Tote
Fearnmore
Rubha Chuaig
Fearnbeg
Arinacrinachd
ISLAND OF RONA
Cuaig
Kenmore
Eilean Garbh
Creag a' Lain
1995
Beinn a' Sgà
Callakille
Eilean Tigh
Garbh Eilean
THE STORR
2358
Old Man of Storr
Bearreraig Bay
Ard na Claise Móire
Lonbain
Eyre
Kensaleyre
Beinn a' Chearcaill
1812
Holm Island
Eilean Fladday
Loch Leathan
Loch Fada
Manish Point
Prince Charles's Cave
Tote
Carbost
Borve
Arnish
Brochel
2053
Beinn a' Chlachain
Drumuie
Achachork
1288
Rubha na h-Airde Glaise
Glengrasco
Torvaig
Applecross House
Applecross
Portree
Cave
Sgeir Mhór
Udairn
A87
Beinn na Greine
Penifiler
Heatherfield
Ben Tianavaig
1355
1367
Glame
1242
ISLE OF RAASAY
Camusteel
Camusterrach
Glenmore
1300
Stròc-bheinn
Camastianavaig
Balachuirn
Balmeanach
Holoman Bay
1455
Dùn Caan
Ard-dhubh
Culduie
Mugeary
Conordan
Tianavaig Bay
Oskaig
Rubha na' Leac
Eilean na Bà
Toscaig
Lower Ollach
Upper Ollach
Clachan
Glen Varragill
B883
Gedintailor
Narrows of Raasay
Inverarish
North Fearns
Eilean Beag
1442
Roineval
Meall an Fhuarain
The Braes
Balmeanach
Suisnish Hill
Eyre Point
Eilean Meadhonach
Eilean Mór
Ben Lee
Peinchorran
1456
Ferry
Rubh' an Tòrra Mhóir
Caol Mór
Sgeir Thraid
Sgeir Dhearg
CROWLIN ISLANDS
SCALPAY
Crossal
A863
A87
Sconser
Longay
21
18
23
LAMAIG
930
Sligachan Hotel
Mullach na Càrn
1298
Scalpay House
Black Islands
8
Beinn Bhreac
Loch Ainort
Luib
Dunan
Guillamon Island
91
Pabay
Plock of Kyle
Caolas Scalpay
Sgurr nan Gillean
3167
Glas Bheinn Mhórn
1852
A87
Kyleakin
Marsco
2414
Broadford Bay
Corry
Drochaid Lusa
Beinn na Crò
Beinn na Caillich
2403
11
Breakish
Sgurr a' Ghreadaidh
3197
Harta Corrie
2649
Garbh-bheinn
26
Broadford
Harrapool
Skulamus
Glen Arroch
CUILLIN HILLS
3046
BLA BHEINN
17
A851
9
10
Glenbrittle House
Sgurr Alasdair
3257
3037
Sgurr nan Eag
Torrin
Kilbride
Sgurr na Stri
1623
Strathaird
25
Beinn nan Càrn
983
Kinloch
Beinn na Seamraig
Ceann na Beinne
736
Kirkibost
Kilmarie
13
908
Heaste
Cairn
Dun
Ulfhart Point
Loch Scavaig
Dun Ringill
Eilean Heast
Drumfearn
SOAY SOUND
Beinn Bhreac
464
An Dubh-laimhrig
Ben Meabost
1128
Rubha Suisnish
Ardnameacon
Leac nam Faoileann
307
SOAY
Port na Cullaidh
Loch Eishort
Sgòrach Breac
981
Ord
Duisdalemore
Elgol
Dunsgiath Castle
Isleomsay or Eilean Iarmain
Ornsay
Na Gamhnaichean
Prince Charles's Cave
Glasnakille
Dun Grugaig
Camus Croise
Rubha na h-Easgainne
Eilean na h-Airde
Tokavaig
Tarskavaig Point
Tarskavaig
Sgurr na h-Iolaire
959
Teangue
Achnacloich
Saasaig
Rubha Ard Slisneach
Knock Bay
Ferindonald
818
Kilmore
Kilbeg
Rubha Shamhnan
Inver Dalavil
Gleann Meadhonach
Armadale Castle
Armadale Bay
Camas Pliasgaig
Rubha Charn nan Cearc
Sgurr nan Caorach
920
Ardvasar
Calligarry
An Fhaochag
Sandaig
12
Geur Rubha
Aird of Sleat
30 mins
Rubha na Roinne
Loch Scresort
Ard Thurinish
Glas Eilean
Kinloch
Rubha Port na Caranean
Point of Sleat
Rubha Raonuill
Sgurr-an Eilein Ghiubhais
664
Mallaig
Mallaig Bheag
1713
1796
RUM
A830
1444
SOUND OF RAASAY
INNER SOUND
SOUND OF SLEAT
ISLE OF SKYE

Keymap

SCALE 1:294 118 or 1 INCH to about 4¾ MILES *1CM to 2.9KM*

0 2 4 6 8 10 KILOMETRES 15

0 2 4 6 MILES 8 10

KEYMAP HEIGHTS SHOWN IN FEET

At-a-glance...

Walk	Page	Start	Nat. Grid Reference	Distance	Time	Highest Point
Acairseid an Rubha	34	Aird of Sleat	NG 588007	3½ miles (5.8km)	2½ hrs	345ft (105m)
Balmacara to Kyle of Lochalsh	20	Balmacara Square	NG 807283	3½ miles (5.6km)	2 hrs	590ft (180m)
Balmacara Woodland Walk	24	Balmacara Square	NG 807283	3½ miles (5.7km)	2 hrs	655ft (200m)
Bealach an Sgairne	57	Morvich	NG 961211	8 miles (13km)	4 hrs	1722ft (525m)
Ben Aslak	30	Bealach Udal, Kylerhea Glen	NG 755207	3 miles (5km)	2 hrs	2000ft (610m)
Bla Bheinn	46	Loch Slapin	NG 561215	5 miles (8km)	4-5 hrs	3044ft (928m)
Broadford coast and forest walk	32	Broadford	NG 643235	5 miles (8km)	2½ hrs	50ft (15m)
Bruach na Frithe	60	Sligachan	NG 479298	8 miles (13km)	5-6 hrs	3143ft (958m)
Caisteal Grùgain (Totaig Broch)	22	Letterfearn	NG 884239	3½ miles (5.8km)	2 hrs	165ft (50m)
Camasunary	36	Kilmarie	NG 545172	2½ miles (4km) (each way)	2½ hrs	620ft (189m)
Drumbuie Croft	12	Duirinish Station	NG 778315	1½ miles (2.5km)	1½ hrs	65ft (20m)
Duncraig Hill	42	Achnandarach	NG 803314	5¼ (8.5km)	2-3 hrs	1125ft (343m)
Gleann Beag	80	Eilanreach or Balvraid	NG 808180 or NG 847165	12 miles (19km) or 5½ miles (9km)	3-6 hrs	712ft (217m)
Gleann Lichd	63	Morvich	NG 961211	8 miles (12.8km)	4 hrs	165ft (50m)
Glen Sligachan	49	Sligachan	NG 487299	7¾ miles (12.5km)	4-5 hrs	278ft (85m)
Into Glen Affric	84	Loch Cluanie	NG 092121	15 miles (24km)	8 hrs	1325ft (404m)
Kylerhea Trail	18	Kylerhea Otter Centre	NG 786210	3 miles (4.5km)	1½ hrs	165ft (50m)
Kylerhea Glen circuit	70	Kylerhea Otter Centre	NG 786210	8¾ miles (14km)	5-6 hrs	2424ft (739m)
Loch Achaidh na h-Inich	40	Balmacara Square	NG 807283	5 miles (8km)	2-3 hrs	655ft (200m)
Loch Alsh	53	Glenelg ferry car park	NG 795214	7¾ (12.5km)	4-5 hrs	755ft (230m)
Loch Scalpaidh	26	Kyle of Lochalsh	NG 761273	3¾ miles (6km)	2 hrs	426ft (130m)
Marsco	67	Sligachan	NG 487299	8 miles (13km)	5 hrs	2415ft (736m)
Sandaig	14	Upper Sandaig	NG 784152	2¾ miles (4.5km)	1½ hrs	375ft (115m)
Sgurr an Airgid	44	Clachan Duich, Morvich	NG 946212	6¼ miles (10km)	3-4 hrs	2759ft (841m)
Sgurr na Coinnich	28	Bealach Udal, Kylerhea Glen	NG 755207	2¼ miles (4km)	2 hrs	2424ft (739m)
Shieldaig	16	Shieldaig	NG 815539	3 miles (4.7km)	2 hrs	85ft (30m)
Srath Mór and Srath Beag	77	Torrin	NG 565224	10½ (17km)	5-6 hrs	623 ft (190m)
Suisnish and Boreraig	73	Kilchrist (Cill Chriosd), Strath Suardal	NG 617207	10 miles (16km)	5 hrs	525ft (160m

Comments
A chance to explore the southern reaches of Skye, and the fecund scenery of Sleat, the so-called Garden of Skye, on this rough little walk.
Following much of the former track that linked Balmacara and Kyle of Lochalsh in the days before the modern road, this route offers splendid views and some lovely old trees.
This is a delightful forest walk combining both spruce plantation and native oak and beech woodland. Lovely open sections provide charming views of the hills of Skye, Loch Alsh and Kyle Rhea.
Known as 'The Gates of Affric' the Bealach an Sgairne offers a demanding but rewarding trek deep into the folds of high mountains.
A short sharp pull over heathery terrain leads to a fine viewpoint, and a surprise lochan.
A long and demanding ascent to arguably the finest mountain summit on Skye; all the effort is generously rewarded with a bird's-eye view of the Black Cuillin and the great Glen Sligachan
A delightful walk along the coast from Broadford, exploring the basaltic geology before turning into a small plantation and retreating to Broadford along the old road.
A demanding but rewarding ascent to the Cuillin ridge, across rugged terrain. Clear visibility is needed, along with stamina and a head for heights.
An easy, out-and-back walk along the shores of Loch Duich to a 2000-year old settlement. A wonderful walk for wildlife, flowers and trees.
An easy walk to one of the finest 'surprise' views on Skye, and a bay of enchantment. Choose a clear, warm day and take a picnic.
A brief but interesting walk that visits traditional farming sites and coastal waters frequented by otters. There is also an abundance of wild flowers.
A fine circular walk leading to a craggy summit with an outstanding viewpoint, set amid a troubled landscape of hills and hollows and reedy lakes.
An easy walk into a verdant glen filled with pre- and latter-day history. The walk can be shortened by driving to Balvraid, but there is much to commend walking the whole distance, in and out.
An easy, but longish walk into a beautiful and remote glen, flanked by high mountains. Good tracks all the way and the chance to spot a golden eagle or red deer.
A long linear walk through the finest glen on Skye. More walking (2 ½ miles/4km) is needed at the end of it to return to civilisation. A spectacular and awe-inspiring route.
A long and demanding linear walk through high mountains and glens: very remote and requiring experience in rugged terrain.
A chance to spot otters in their natural habitat, and to enjoy an easy walk above the narrow sound of Kyle Rhea.
A rough, tough demanding walk suitable only for strong and experienced walkers tackling it on a good day. The views are superb, and the company likely to be non-existent.
Walk through birch and willow woodland to a peaceful loch set amid low craggy hills from which the views are ever-changing as the walk progresses.
An energetic exploration of the stunning coastline of Kyle Rhea and Loch Alsh preludes a speedy return across mountainous terrain with outstanding views for company.
Lost among heathery hummocks, lonely Loch Scalpaidh makes a splendid objective for a short walk from Kyle. Although only a short way from civilisation, this loch seems very remote.
A strenuous and steep climb to one of Skye's most distinctive summits, which serves as a stunning viewpoint that makes the effort well worthwhile.
A poignant and evocative visit to the place made eternally popular by Gavin Maxwell, Sandaig, which he called Camusfeàrna, the Bay of the Alders.
A demanding and rather tough little climb to a fabulous vantage point with far-reaching views. Anything less than a clear day would be pointless.
A tough, pathless climb across difficult terrain to a remote summit with a fabulous panorama. This is a walk for connoisseurs.
With the huge panoply of Applecross and Torridon as a backdrop, this easy and brief walk explores the headland north of the tiny village of Shieldaig.
Two demanding glen walks combine in this circuit of Beinn na Cro, that needs dry conditions for successful completion. Even so, expect some boggy going.
A long and delightful walk underpinned by a sorrowful episode in the history of the Isle of Skye. Easy tracks, good paths and trails lead to a fine moorland crossing.

Introduction to Kyle of Lochalsh

This Pathfinder Guide is centred on the small town of Kyle of Lochalsh from where a bridge now links the mainland of Scotland to the Isle of Skye. All the walks begin within about an hour's travel by road from Kyle, and they range from easy coastal walks through crofting land to the high mountains of the Cuillin on Skye and Kintail. Just under half of the walks are on Skye, while most of the rest tend to lie eastwards of Kyle, into the area known as Kintail.

There is an easy division between the type of routes, which are either coastal (or near coastal) or into mountainous terrain. It is among the 'mountainous' selection of walks that the greatest diversity appears, with the walks ranging from demanding ascents in the Black and Red Cuillin to valley routes both on Skye and among the mountains of Kintail. Some of the walks are extremely rugged, and involve trekking across untracked hillsides where the ability to navigate accurately is essential to success. Walks in this category demand proper equipment and clothing and some experience of hard walking: they are intended to whet the appetite of visitors to the region, and to encourage them to explore independently. Elsewhere, the walks visit what I can only describe as corners of Heaven set aside for lovers of solitude and the simple pleasures of Nature: the sort of places where you might well perch beside a mountain loch watching damselflies going about their business or a grey heron on the lookout for lunch, and become so at one with the setting that you may well not wish to leave. The sound of silence can be a very persuasive argument, and the company of solitude among the most forceful of reasons for seeking out Kintail's quiet corners.

The Skye Bridge from Kyle of Lochalsh

Skye and Kintail both have their unique identities, historically, geographically and geologically, and they possess some of the most breathtaking landscapes in Britain. Here the walking is good at all times of year, but the prevailing climate imposes some strict conditions on access that can, and

Balmacara woodland

should, deter walkers without commensurate experience. Given proper clothing and equipment, however, even a torrential downpour in Glen Sligachan on Skye or a wind-battered trek into Glen Affric and out through Gleann Lichd can provide an exhilarating and robust day, and add immeasurably to one's experience and pleasure. My own first experience of Glen Sligachan (in 1983) was much as described, but it was with inordinate inner satisfaction that I perched on a boulder beside Loch an Athain and munched a tin of mandarin oranges as raindrops kept falling from my nose. Of course, none of the ascents to high mountain tops is to be undertaken by anyone in poor conditions, and, in winter, may well be out of reach altogether.

Walkers whose only experience of walking has been on lowland landscapes where paths are clear and plentiful or where guidebooks give detailed route descriptions will almost certainly find the area covered by this book something of an eye-opener. Here, some self-reliance is called for from time to time. The ruggedness of the terrain on some of the walks and the remoteness from outside help make this a place where ambition needs wise counsel and the consequences of 'getting it wrong' far more serious. If conditions are poor, chill out, relax, and wait for things to improve before setting off. Certainly none of the first eight walks in the book is likely to cause undue problems in any conditions, although getting to the start of some of them could be difficult if snow is at a low level. But the rest need a careful assessment of weather conditions, proper equipment including sturdy boots and a rucksack to carry waterproofs, spare clothes, refreshments, maps and compass. Even the driest of the walks can be very wet after prolonged rain, and, in Scotland, the rain knows how to prolong, but, to be fair, the sun knows how to shine, too.

Few of the walks are day-long outings, most can probably be accomplished in a matter of hours, allowing time to visit other places of interest. Some are linear, and this will mean resolving the transport problem: two cars are one solution, getting a lift or using public transport (including the post bus) are others. Some walks are intentionally 'out-and-back', but most present a completely different set of images on the return journey: others are of variable length – go as far as you want, and then come back.

Rugged as it may seem, most of the land explored in these walks is used for agricultural purposes, making it especially important to close gates, avoid climbing over fences, especially high deer fences, and not to invade the privacy of the people who live and work here. Deer stalking is an important part of the local economy, a pursuit that occurs from mid-August usually until about mid-October. Few of the walks in this book are likely to be affected by this, but if any become affected it is usual for notices to be posted at access points asking walkers to refrain from entering the area. This restriction rarely exceeds a day or so.

Dogs, even dogs under control, tend not to be welcome during lambing time, between mid-April and early June. At other times, all dogs should be permanently on leads and not allowed to run free over hillsides or through pastures. The number of places where dogs are banned is increasing, but, at the time of writing (September 2002) very few in this book are affected.

What many visitors will find fascinating is the incredible richness of wild flowers that prevail here, even high up on mountainsides where I have

The final pull to the top of Duncraig Hill

Ruminant inhabitant of the Shieldaig headland

found heath spotted orchids growing in late September. Around the coasts it is the sealife – birds and mammals – that will astound. Nothing will be seen by the noisy visitor, of course, but a quiet approach anywhere could well reward with the sight of deer, an otter, grey or Atlantic seals, whales (even killer whales have been known), porpoise and dolphin, with eagles, golden and white-tailed, appearing overhead.

One final comment concerns the predominance of three wee human-feasting beasties that are an annoyance to everyone: ticks tend to be found in bracken and dense vegetation; clegs, horseflies intent on aggravating anyone who comes near them and with a ferocious bite, occur everywhere, and then there is the midge, a peculiarly persistent pest that gathers in clouds and munches companionably on all the repellents, creams, lotions and potions used to deter them, generally retreating only in the face of high winds and rain. All of these occur from June until September, but, as the climate has warmed in recent times, this period seems to be expanding.

Setting aside these relatively minor irritations, the walking in the area covered by this book ranks among the best in Scotland. There is a good cross-section of walks to give a taste of everything, and something to satisfy everyone. By the time you have discovered the superb restaurants selling local seafood and produce, and the conviviality of the numerous pubs and inns, you may well be forgiven for thinking there is nowhere on earth quite so good.

• *Glossary of Gaelic words – page 92*

Drumbuie Croft

Start	Duirinish Railway Station
Distance	$1\frac{1}{2}$ miles (2.5km)
Approximate time	$1\frac{1}{2}$ hours
Parking	Near station (limited)
Refreshments	Kyle of Lochalsh
Ordnance Survey maps	Landranger 24 (Raasay, Applecross & Loch Torridon), Explorer 428 (Kyle of Lochalsh, Plockton & Applecross)

This brief walk crosses flower-rich croftland at the sea's edge. Port an-eorna was returned to active crofting in 1996, and, close by, runrig strips of cultivated land from earlier crofting episodes are also visible. The combination of sea and coastal farmlands is peaceful and relaxing, and the abundance of wild flowers in summer sure to make this modest outing one of great pleasure.

There is limited parking near the railway station at Duirinish, and from here turn past the railway cottages to reach a broad grassy track leading to a stile over a fence. Beyond, head slightly downhill to cross another fence, the route having occasional waymarks for the 'Coastal Walk'. At the second fence, turn right and follow it across more stiles and a bridge to reach the village of Drumbuie **A**.

The tiny enclave of Drumbuie is a delightful, almost random, scattering of

0 200 400 600 800 METRES 1 KILOMETRES
0 200 400 600 YARDS ½ MILES

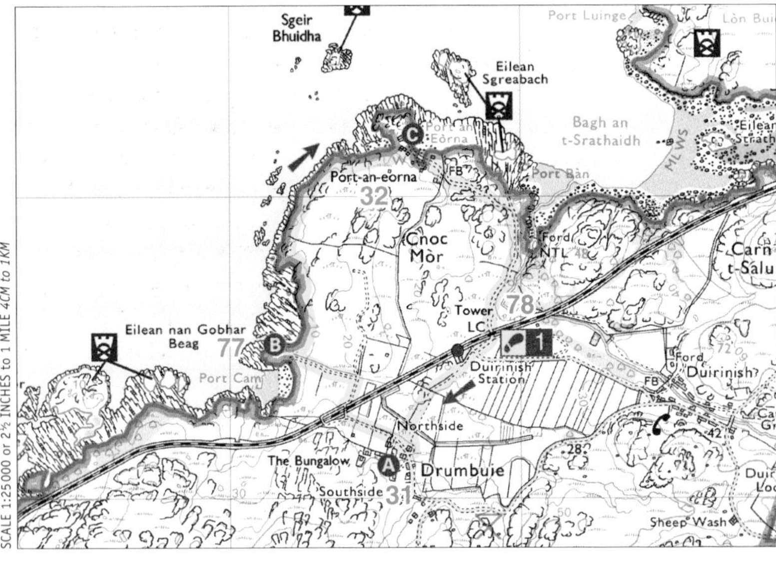

SCALE 1:25 000 or $2\frac{1}{2}$ INCHES to 1 MILE 4CM to 1KM

Cottage, Port an-eorna

cottages and houses tucked snugly into the landscape. Follow the road through it to a gate near a large agricultural shed. Through the gate, follow the on-going track beside which there are examples of runrig cultivation.

Runrig is a system of community farming on arable land under which, traditionally, strips of ground were apportioned by lot on an annual or triennial basis. When the land was divided, a portion was always set aside for the landless, known in Scotland as *cionagan nam bochd*, the plots of the poor (a *cionag* was ¼ *cliteag*, or ¼ feorling, i.e. 'farthing land'). Because the land was poorly drained, either by landform or neglect, cultivation was generally undertaken in long narrow strips running parallel with the slope of the land. These allotments, or 'beds', were traditionally about 2 yds (1.75m) wide, divided from each other by a trough about 1ft deep and 2 ft wide. Under this form of multiple lazy bed (termed *feannagan taomaidh*), the ground was invariably dry for the growing crop, usually potatoes, though oats, barley and turnips were also grown.

Cross the railway, and go left on a small track, following the field boundary to the shore Ⓑ. The route passes along the edge of an area planted with yellow flag iris, and where a host of flowers grow in summer including the butterfly orchid. The area is especially popular with seabirds and otters, and attempts are being made to re-establish corncrakes in the area. The corncrake is an infuriating bird: its voice is a determined and rasping 'crex-crex', which it repeats sometimes for hours on end, yet it is virtually impossible to spot one, leading some to suggest that the corncrake has ventriloquial abilities.

At the shoreline, at a small rocky bay, bear right and follow the coastline, on an indistinct path, to a stile spanning a fence, beyond which lies the small township of Port an-eorna (Barley Port) Ⓒ, reached by a narrow path. At a road, turn right and follow this to a double-gated level crossing. Over this, bear right with the surfaced lane back to Duirinish station. ●

Sandaig

Start	Upper Sandaig
Distance	2¾ miles (4.5km)
Approximate time	1½ hours
Parking	Near Loch Drabhaig
Refreshments	Glenelg
Ordnance Survey maps	Landranger 33 (Loch Alsh, Glen Shiel & Loch Hourn), Explorer 413 (Knoydart, Loch Hourn & Loch Duich)

Sooner or later devotees of the writings of Gavin Maxwell, author of the world-famous book Ring of Bright Water, *will find their way to his Highland retreat, Sandaig, which he called Camusfeàrna. Hidden from view by a cloak of pine, the 'Bay of the Alders' nestles between the mainland and the embracing arm of the scattered Sandaig Islands. It is, for everyone who knows the story, a poignant and evocative place, where the sounds of Nature – the ripple of the burn, the harsh 'kraak' of a heron, or the soft, plaintive song of a seal out among the rocks – are all that disturb the heavy mantle of tranquillity. This walk descends through the blanket of woodland to find this pilgrim's Mecca, and in doing so steps back to a time when Man and a wild animal wove a story of unimaginable intrigue.*

Gavin Maxwell, according to his biographer, Douglas Botting, was to otters what Joy Adamson was to lions, or Dian Fossey to gorillas; his relationship with red deer, grouse and basking sharks was, some would say, less commendable. But he was a most gifted writer, an eccentric, a romantic, a painter, poet and journalist – he was, too, a secret agent, a racing driver and very much a social misfit.

The visit to Sandaig, an out-and-back walk, begins along the narrow road from Glenelg to Arnisdale, close by the reed-lined Loch Drabhaig. Here turn off the road, around a metal barrier and onto a broad track descending gently into the plantation that swathes the seaward slopes overlooking the hills of Sleat. Well-established now, the plantation holds luxuriant growths of moss, ferns and fungi through which the track falls steadily in loops to cross the Allt Mór Shantaig. On the other side, the track rises to a cleared area and track 'crossroads' **A**. Here turn sharp right, descending around a few more bends.

Keep an eye open for a distinct, wide track branching right, as the main trail bears left. Turn onto this, following it as it winds a way down through what must have been the original woodland that shielded Camusfeàrna from the outside world. The descending track eventually reaches a gate giving onto

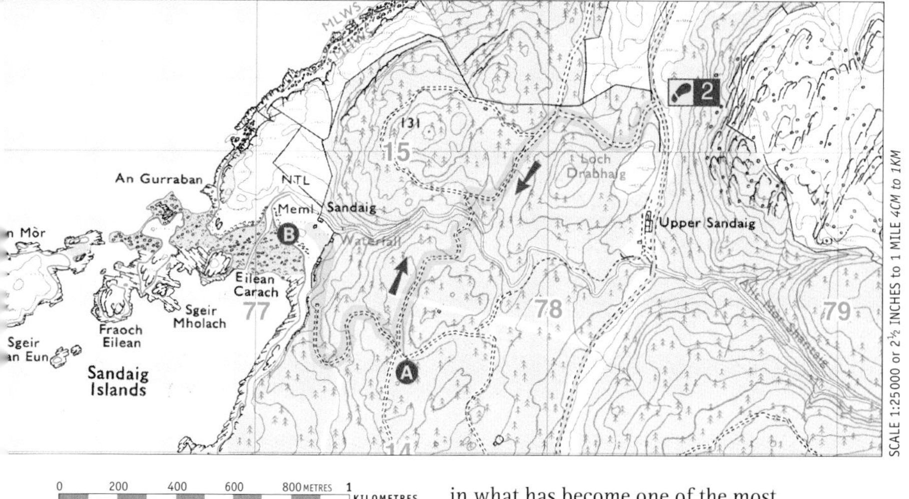

the flat, coastal meadowland at Sandaig, close by a white croft **B**. And around it all, the burn that was the 'ring of bright water'.

In the middle, where once stood Maxwell's house, now stands a memorial boulder and plaque marking the spot where his ashes were buried. Nearby, closer to the burn it frequented so often, another memorial stone commemorates Edal, the otter of the *Ring of Bright Water.* A ford by the burn can usually be crossed to walk a short way around the tiny headland, but for most visitors it is fitting simply to be in what has become one of the most unexpected pilgrimage sites of modern times, just as Gavin Maxwell had wanted.

Many a love affair with the natural history of the Scottish islands has been inspired by the writings of Gavin Maxwell, and his hauntingly perceptive account of life at the far outer edge of mainstream and aristocratic society. The man lived a comparatively brief and difficult life: he was aged 55 when he died in 1969, probably of natural causes, although both suicide and euthanasia have been suggested.

The return journey simply retraces the outward route back to the start of the walk.

The bay at Sandaig

Shieldaig

Start	Shieldaig
Distance	3 miles (4.7km)
Approximate time	2 hours
Parking	Shieldaig
Refreshments	Shieldaig (hotel), Kyle of Lochalsh, Plockton
Ordnance Survey maps	Landranger 24 (Raasay, Applecross & Loch Torridon), Explorer 428 (Kyle of Lochalsh, Plockton & Applecross)

The coastal scenery around Shieldaig is among the finest in Scotland, and few places can be better perched to observe it than the small community of Shieldaig. This short walk, almost in the shadow of Torridon's mighty Munros, though rugged in places, tours the headland north of Shieldaig, providing constantly changing views of lochs and mountains.

Begin at the war memorial, a latter-day loose link with the reason the village of Shieldaig was founded, in 1800, as a training base for seamen being sent to fight in the war against Napoleon. Sadly, having enticed seafaring men and their families to live in Shieldaig by means of incentives, when the war was over, the assistance ended and the men and their families

A small group of puffins on the headland at Shieldaig

were left to look after themselves. Fortune, however, smiled on the brave, for the coastal waters were full of fish, enough certainly to sustain this infant community. Today, with much of the worthwhile fishing gone, the village has to rely on tourism, and walkers who visit to stroll around the headland.

Walk down to the school and bear right, ignoring the driveway to Rubha Lodge. The on-going path is agreeable walking, undulating easily through trees to arrive at an open grassy area near a stony beach. From here the path soon reaches a cairn Ⓐ, where it forks. Branch left onto a meandering path that pokes into numerous nooks and crannies suitable for a picnic, and from which there are memorable views of Applecross and the hills of Torridon.

At its northern end, the path leads to a cottage Ⓑ overlooking the tiny, rocky islet Eilean a'Chaoil, and here turns east to cross a stretch of open moorland to a rocky stairway leading to the isolated cottage at Bad-callda.

From the cottage the path now heads south, crossing a section of bare rock to another rocky stairway overlooking the tiny Camas an Léim Ⓒ, a beautiful spot to while away time.

Onwards, the path threads through heather and finally reaches the cairn at which the outward path divided. From here simply retrace the outward route back to Shieldaig.

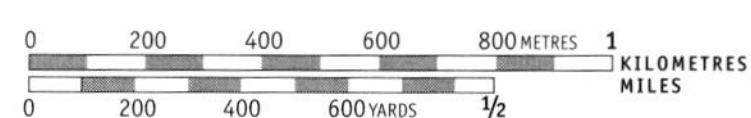

SCALE 1:25 000 or 2½ INCHES to 1 MILE 4CM to 1KM

Kylerhea Trail

Start	Kylerhea
Distance	3 miles (4.5km)
Approximate time	1½ hours
Parking	Kylerhea Otter Centre
Refreshments	Broadford, Glenelg
Ordnance Survey maps	Landranger 33 (Loch Alsh, Glen Shiel & Loch Hourn), Explorer 413 (Knoydart, Loch Hourn & Loch Duich)

As with so many walks around the west coast of Scotland, binoculars are part of the essential equipment every walker should take. The area around Kylerhea (pronounced Kile-ray) is especially popular with otters, and here Forest Enterprise have set up a viewing hide overlooking the kyle. If otters are not readily on view, seals – common and Atlantic grey – and seabirds almost invariably are. Patience and silence are essential prerequisites if otters are to be seen. This short walk visits the hide and then performs a loop through typical otter terrain before returning. Dogs are not allowed on the trail; the scent of a dog can disturb the wildlife of the area.

Otters are members of the Mustelidae family, which includes weasel, stoat and mink, and an average sized otter will measure about 4 ft (1.2m). They will eat anything, and have a hearty appetite, though their main diet comprises fish,

Kylerhea woodlands from the trail

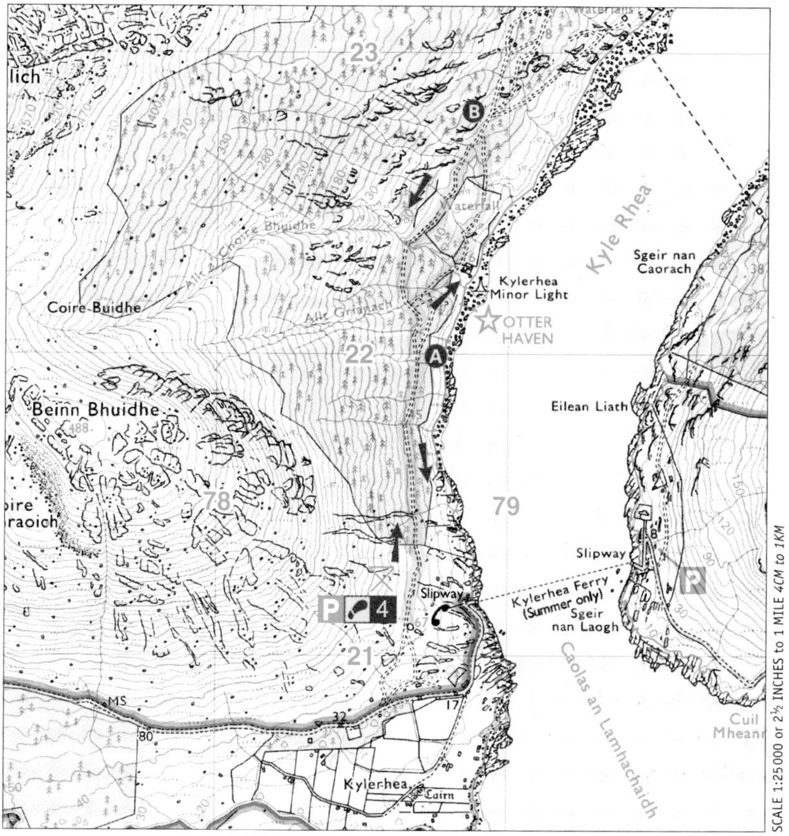

SCALE 1:25 000 or 2½ INCHES to 1 MILE *4CM to 1KM*

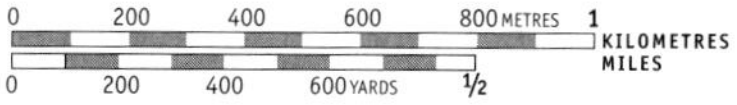

crustaceans, amphibians and small mammals. Otters are a protected species under the Wildlife and Countryside Act 1981, under the provisions of which it is an offence intentionally to disturb an otter in its place of shelter, or knowingly to approach its holt.

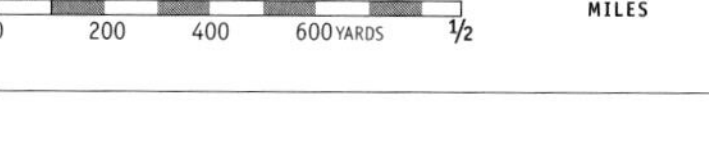

The start of the walk is found not far from the Kylerhea ferry slip, at the far end of Kylerhea Glen, reached by a narrow and circuitous route through a fascinating landscape from the main Kyleakin - Broadford road.

Leave the car park, following the broad trail, and soon pass through a gate giving access to the nature reserve (toilets here). There are throughout the walk great views across the kyle to the wooded slopes of Druim na Leitire.

On approaching the viewing hide (A), keep as quiet as possible, otherwise any chance of seeing otters, or anything else for that matter, will vanish. The hide is usually manned by Forest Enterprise, who can give advice on what to look for, as will the displays within the hide.

On leaving the hide, turn right descending onto a wooded trail for a short detour, past a miniature waterfall and pool, then climb steps back onto the main trail (B). *Turn left for a quick return to the start*; otherwise go right and follow the trail until it ends, close by overhead powerlines.

Go back to the car park along the main trail, scanning the heathery slopes of Beinn Bhuidhe for a glimpse of red deer or a patrolling golden eagle.

Balmacara to Kyle of Lochalsh

Start	Balmacara Square
Distance	3½ miles (5.6km)
Approximate time	2 hours
Parking	Balmacara Square
Refreshments	Balmacara, Kyle of Lochalsh
Ordnance Survey maps	Landranger 33 (Loch Alsh, Glen Shiel & Loch Hourn), Explorer 413 (Knoydart, Loch Hourn & Loch Duich)

A delightful walk with panoramic views over Loch Alsh to the Skye hills. The route begins in the restored township of Balmacara Square, and sets off along what was the old route to Kyle in the days before the roadway was built. It passes through some lovely native woodland, and above the abandoned settlement of Scalpaidh before heading down to Kyle of Lochalsh.

This linear walk will need the problems of transport resolving, either by using two cars, or by taking the bus back from Kyle to Balmacara Square (or vice versa, taking the bus to Balmacara Square first). The possibility of simply walking back to Balmacara Square after refreshments in Kyle should not be discounted. This is a delightful walk, and tackling it in both directions is unlikely to prove a hardship and not at all repetitive.

Begin from the parking area in Balmacara Square and turn right as if heading for the main road, but, opposite a broad track on the left after about 440 yds (400m), leave the road by branching right into dense pine

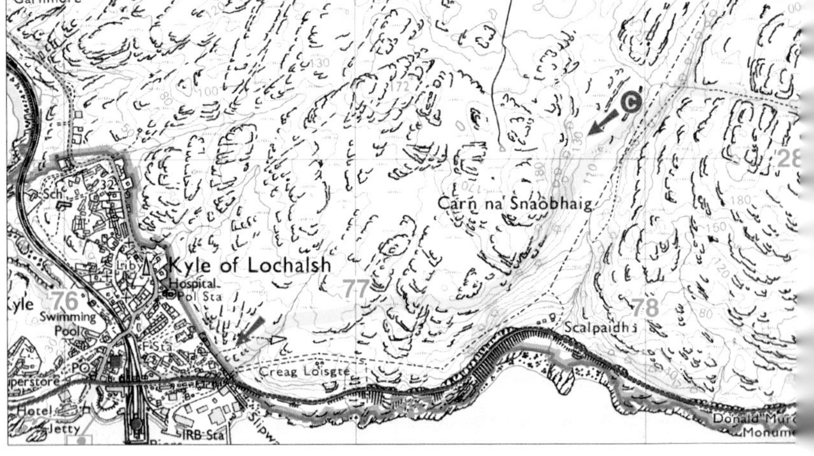

woodland onto a route waymarked by poles banded with red and green. Follow the track through the plantation, which crosses the second road into Balmacara Square Ⓐ.

Continue into more woodland for a while on a good track, the original route between Balmacara and Kyle. There are some fine old beeches here and a number of stiles across fences throughout the first part of the walk.

The native distribution of the magnificent beech tree is confined to southern England, but throughout Britain it has naturalised successfully and is well established everywhere. The name 'beech' is thought to derive from an Anglo-Saxon word 'boc', which in turn produced 'book'. Some forms of early book used thin strips of beech into which the writing would be carved. The beech has been valued as fuel since Roman times, but it has also been used extensively for the manufacture of furniture, tools and buckets.

Cross a deer fence surrounding a larch plantation and head into an area of young Scots pine. Beyond this another fence awaits, but then, once clear of the woodland, the path strikes out across open moorland.

The route leads through a gap in an old dyke Ⓑ and then across a heather-covered slope, where ling, bell heather and cross-leaved heath all flourish. Cross a burn and press on to a crosspath Ⓒ at the top of the walk from Scalpaidh Bay to Loch Scalpaidh.

A signpost indicates the continuing route to Kyle of Lochalsh, which follows a delightful course, for quite some time steadily downhill through lichened birch, amid rocky outcrops and with snapshots of Loch Alsh coming and going at gaps through the tree canopy. This is a memorably pleasant stretch, though there is little fault to be found with any of the walk; perhaps just the rusted intrusion of the remains of the pipeline that once supplied Kyle with water from Loch Scalpaidh.

A brief rise leads out of the woodland cover and into a rough and tumble interlude of heather and crags, still largely following the old pipeline, though most of it is buried.

Eventually the path leads into the top end of an old enclosure, and through this descends steeply through gorse, finally emerging into the edge of a small housing estate. Go forward into Langland's Terrace, and then turn right along the main road to reach Kyle. ●

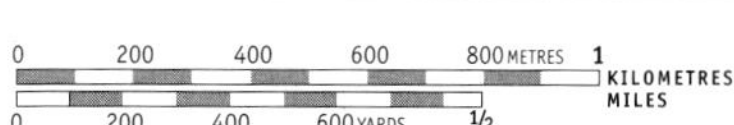

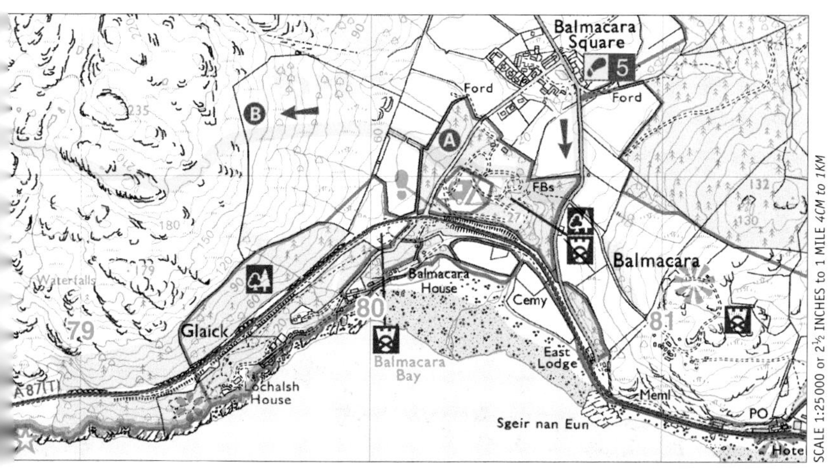

Caisteal Grùgain (Totaig Broch)

Start	Letterfearn
Distance	$3\frac{1}{2}$ miles (5.8km)
Approximate time	2 hours
Parking	Letterfearn (limited, please park considerately)
Refreshments	Shiel Bridge, Dornie
Ordnance Survey maps	Landranger 33 (Loch Alsh, Glen Shiel & Loch Hourn), Explorer 413 (Knoydart, Loch Hourn & Loch Duich)

A modest amount of road walking is the price to be paid for the pleasure of strolling along the west shores of Loch Duich; hard surfaced it may be, but the lochside's natural theatre in which all the cast are feathered or aquatic or both puts on a daily show throughout the year and easily waylays the good intention of visiting the remains of Caisteal Grùgain, a fine broch in a commanding position. Binoculars are essential on this walk.

To make this a fuller day, consider starting as far back as Ratagan Youth Hostel: this will add about 6 miles (9.5km) to the day, but every step is a delight. The lochside is host to a wonderful display of flowers and trees, while the loch itself is frequented by harbour porpoise, cormorant, heron and red-breasted merganser; even pheasants come down to the water's edge to feed.

Eilean Donan Castle

From Letterfearn, simply continue along the surfaced lane, which enters delightful mixed woodland of oak, ash, alder, beech, rowan, larch, Douglas fir, horse chestnut, lime, hazel and sycamore, and finally ends near the Ferry House that once served the Totaig to Dornie ferry **A**.

Conspicuous across the loch is the robust outline of Eilean Donan Castle, probably the most photographed castle in the world. The island on which the castle is built has been a fortified site since the 13th century, though the present building was rebuilt between 1912 and 1932. The Island of Donan is named after a 6th-century Irish saint, Bishop Donan, who came to Scotland in

AD580. More romantically, the island is said to derive from the Gaelic for otter, Cu-Donn, which means brown dog. The story which advances this suggestion describes the King of the Otters, a fine animal recognised by his superb coat of pure silver and white, and tells of his death and how his robe of silver was buried on the island beneath the foundations of the castle.

From the Ferry House, go through a gate onto a dirt track above the water's edge. The track ends at a gate in a deer fence, beyond which a path curves around the edge of a cleared area of forest above a small bay, Ob Inbhir Sgeinnidh **B**. The path starts to climb and then crosses a burn at a shallow ford, after which it reaches the edge of another cleared area, with the ruins of Totaig broch immediately on the left.

The brochs of Iron Age Scotland are distinctive, and architectural masterpieces, built by people who did not possess the technology of later centuries. Yet these fascinating structures were built with such evident precision and skill. Brochs, essentially, are circular drystone fortifications, defence, in the case of Caisteal Grùgain, against marauding rival clans or tribes. They are densely concentrated in the west and north of Scotland, and were probably built about 2000 years ago. Perhaps surprisingly, they remained in use into the second century, and even after that time may well have been the focal point of important settlements for almost 1000 years.

From the broch, simply retrace the outward route.

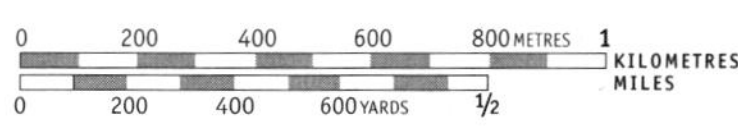

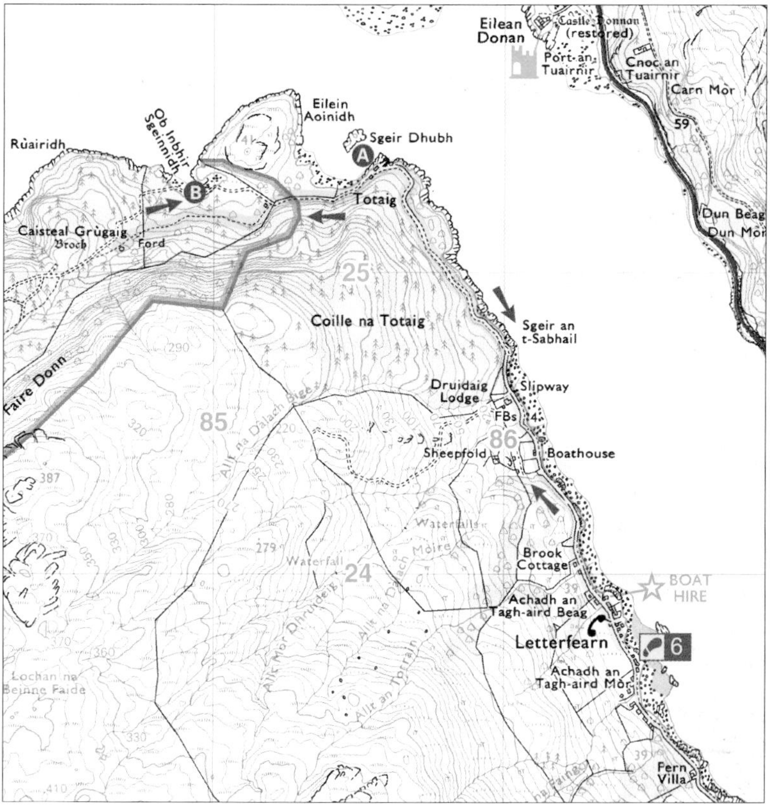

SCALE 1:25 000 or 2½ INCHES to 1 MILE 4CM to 1KM

Balmacara Woodland Walk

Start	Balmacara Square
Distance	3½ miles (5.7km)
Approximate time	2 hours
Parking	Hardwick
Refreshments	Balmacara Square
Ordnance Survey maps	Landranger 33 (Loch Alsh, Glen Shiel & Loch Hourn), Explorer 413 (Knoydart, Loch Hourn & Loch Duich)

For many people, woodland, especially dense conifer plantations, is not the preferred walking habitat, but such places are invariably full of wildlife, seasonally burgeoning with fungi, and in the heat of summer provide welcome shade. The woodlands that flank Sgurr Mór above Balmacara are delightful, and walking routes have been developed through them, combining dark passages of Norway spruce with much lighter, well-established native woodland. This circular walk also provides lovely vistas across Loch Alsh to Kyle Rhea and the hills of Skye.

From the parking area in Balmacara Square turn right following the road as if heading for Balmacara Bay, but only a short way along it, turn left at a kissing-gate onto a signposted 'Forest Walk' that begins around the edge of a paddock. On the far side, another gate gives into pine woodland carpeted with wood sorrel, herb robert, foxgloves and selfheal.

Soon, cross a footbridge, and a short way on, as the track bends right, starting to climb. The route is waymarked throughout by green poles topped with red and/or blue bands: this walk is following the red route – the longer and more demanding of the two, so, once the routes divide, a*nyone wanting a shorter walk can simply follow the blue route.*

The path climbs to meet a broad forest trail Ⓐ. Here turn left, but only for a few strides, as far as a gravel path on the left (waymarked) entering birch and willow woodland popular with members of the tit family, tree creepers, and wrens that fill the burns with their loud and distinctive song. A footbridge, soon reached, spans Balmacara Burn, and then bears right to pass alongside it to another bridge, beyond which the route climbs to a horizontal path. Turn right and walk up to meet the broad forest trail once more.

Throughout this walk the way is littered with the purple-headed flower, devil's-bit scabious, the colour of which can vary from almost white to a deep and intense purple. The plant grows extensively throughout Britain, and was used to produce a concoction to treat snake bites, bad throats and the plague. So successful were the plant's curative properties that, according to herbalist folklore, the Devil bit away part of its

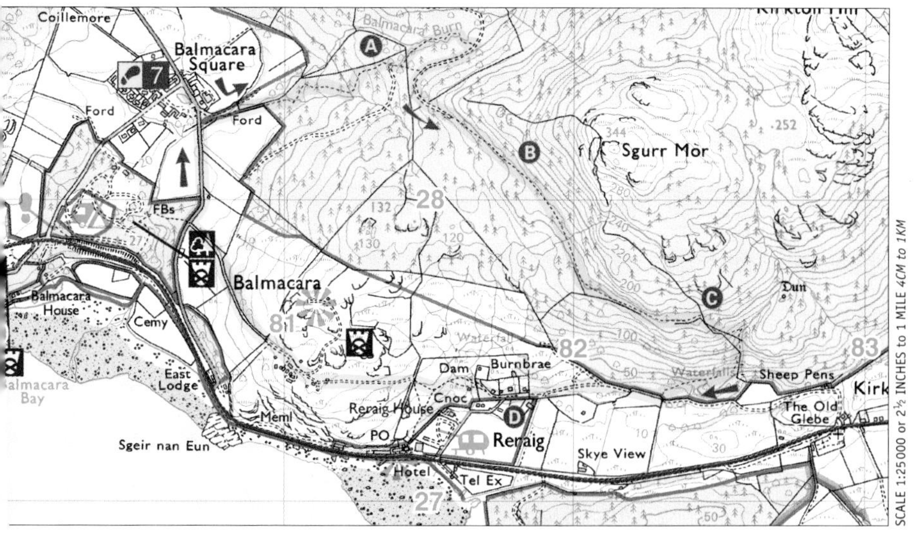

0 200 400 600 800 METRES 1 KILOMETRES
MILES
0 200 400 600 YARDS ½

root in the hope of preventing future growth: on the evidence in Balmacara woodlands (and for that matter just about everywhere covered by this book), his ploy failed.

Cross the broad track and keep forward into dense spruce plantation. The darkness is short-lived, and soon the path eases out into more open woodland of birch, oak and beech. The path forks at a waymark, and close by a stand of beech trees thought to be about 100 years old – so, quite youthful, as beech trees go.

B Branch left, now following the red route, which climbs steadily, passing extensive growths of fungi, *which should not be touched unless someone in the party knows with certainty that it is safe to do so.*

From time to time gaps appear in the tree coverage on the right, allowing cameos of the Kyle hills on Skye, a better view of which appears a short way on at a more open area overlooking Loch Alsh.

The path takes a gently rising route across the southern slope of Sgurr Mór before beginning a descent back into dense woodland, and initially alongside a low dyke heavily embroidered with moss and wood-sorrel.

The descent is short-lived, as the path soon starts to climb again, but only briefly, following which, at the end of the dyke **C**, it turns right and descends very steeply above a wooded gorge and burn. Lower down, the path once more sinks into pine forest through which the route is both waymarked and arrowed.

Eventually, the path descends to meet a broad track almost at the valley bottom. Turn right on this, and on reaching a house, use a signposted gravel path around it, to emerge at the end of a surfaced lane **D**. Go forward, and when the lane forks, branch right, and a short way on, leave it at a footpath sign by branching left onto a grassy path through scrub, to a gate.

The path then climbs gently through gorse and rowan, and when it forks, branch right (signposted for Balmacara Square). Soon, the route climbs to a lovely open terrace with excellent views to the south.

Eventually, the red and blue routes rejoin, continuing forward on a broad stony track flanked by gorse and steadily dropping to meet a road. Turn right to return to Balmacara Square. ●

Loch Scalpaidh

Start	Kyle of Lochalsh
Distance	3¾ miles (6km)
Approximate time	2 hours
Parking	Kyle of Lochalsh
Refreshments	Kyle of Lochalsh
Ordnance Survey maps	Landranger 33 (Loch Alsh, Glen Shiel & Loch Hourn), Explorer 413 (Knoydart, Loch Hourn & Loch Duich)

Lonely Loch Scalpaidh sits in splendid silence among a landscape of heathered hummocks and hollows, a place that once supplied water to Kyle of Lochalsh. Today it hosts red-throated divers, grey herons, myriad damsel- and dragonflies and the occasional patrolling buzzard. There is a direct start from a lay-by at Scalpaigh Bay, but this walk begins in Kyle of Lochalsh in order to take in an old path across the hills.

Leave Kyle along the main road, but soon turn left into Langlands Terrace, taking the first right, a cul-de-sac, that ends at a signpost indicating a path for Balmacara. Set off up this, climbing steadily for a while and being funnelled by the fences of an old enclosure into a narrow passage beyond which a lovely heathery landscape awaits. Much of this early part of the walk follows the course of the water supply pipeline, largely buried, but with enough bits protruding to show its route.

Beyond the hummocky landscape, the path enters birch and oak woodland, and begins a gently undulating but generally ascending trek above Scalpaidh Bay, and finally meets the rising track from the bay, at a signpost near a stile and gate.

A Turn left through the gate and go forward along a muddy path (which at the time of writing, September 2002, was on the brink of improvement) that heads into an avenue of birch trees. The path climbs steadily to the edge of a large heathery hollow, keeping to the left of this to a step-stile spanning a fence, after which it swings left, following the course of a narrow burn.

Loch Scalpaidh and the distant Torridon hills

Soon, the path reaches another hollow **B** carpeted with ling and bog myrtle and with a few willow and rowan dotted about. Edge right around this hollow, heading for a small clump of birch, and soon bringing Loch Scalpaidh into view.

The path seems to end at the loch, but it is possible to complete a circuit, albeit a rough one, following which the return journey simply retraces the outward route.

On the way back there are stunning views across to the hills of Skye, Loch Alsh and Kyle Rhea. Just after the stile/gate **A**, at the signpost above Scalpaidh Bay, the outward route from Kyle lies to the right, but instead make an alternative finish by going forward and descending steeply to discover the remains of the small settlement of Scalpaidh buried amid birch, hazel, rowan and oak just above the main road. Little is known about the settlement, except that its inhabitants did not stay very long. There is no crofting land here, which would have been an important factor, but the likelihood is that the settlement was a temporary development built by people moved from better ground during the time of the Highland Clearances.

Just below the settlement, the descending path emerges at a lay-by. Now turn right and follow the road back to Kyle: there are either good verges or roadside footpaths to maintain a safe distance from approaching traffic, but even so, care is advised.

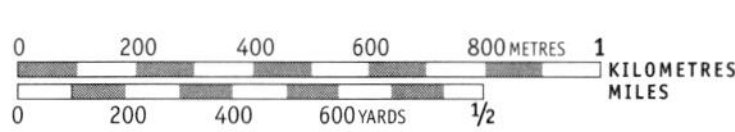

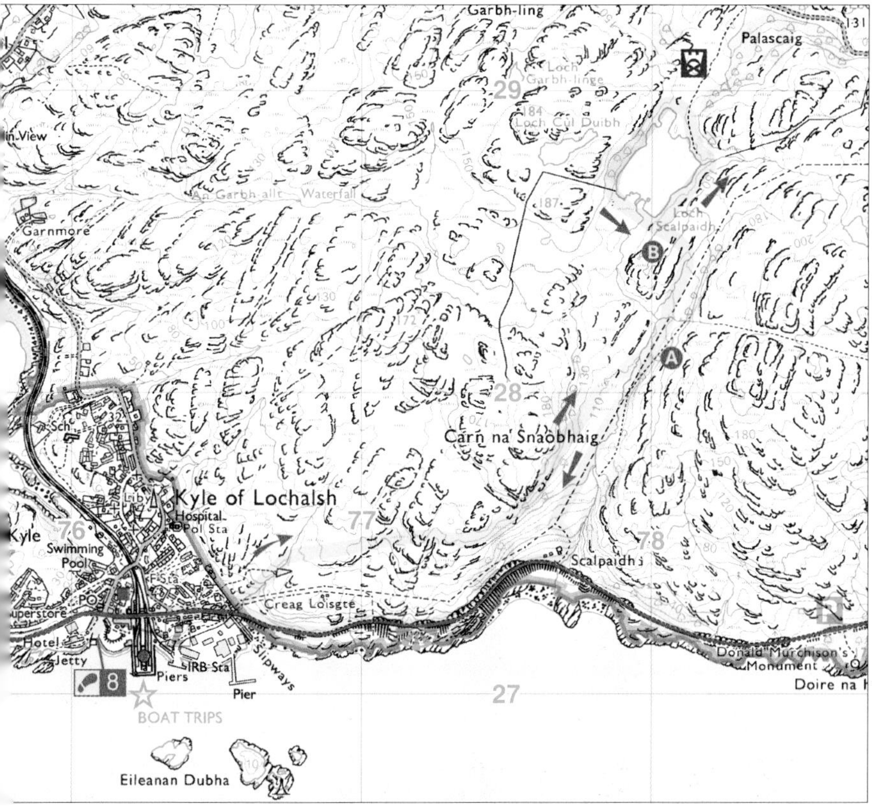

SCALE 1:25000 or 2½ INCHES to 1 MILE *4CM to 1KM*

Sgurr na Coinnich

Start	Bealach Udal
Distance	2¼ miles (4km)
Approximate time	2 hours
Parking	Bealach Udal
Refreshments	Broadford
Ordnance Survey maps	Landranger 33 (Loch Alsh, Glen Shiel & Loch Hourn), Explorer 413 (Knoydart, Loch Hourn & Loch Duich)

There are many mountain summits which, on the face of it, one would never think of ascending, unless prompted. Sgurr na Coinnich is one of these. The ascent from the Bealach Udal, at the head of Kylerhea Glen is tough and steep – craggy outcrops, tussock grass, knee-deep heather, and no evident path. Yet this infrequently visited summit has a panorama that few will have admired, and a remarkable tendency to make visitors linger, sequestered in some rocky embrace, while the world passes by. The effort of getting there is rewarded with smug satisfaction.

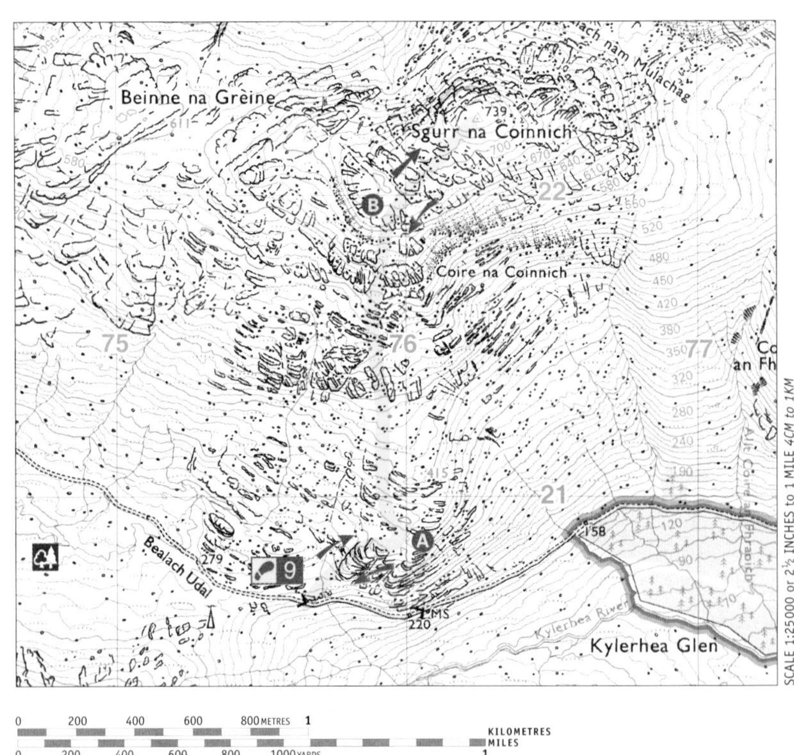

Sgurr na Coinnich and Beinn Bhuidhe

With 1510 ft (460m) of height gain to add insult to the injury of difficult terrain, Sgurr na Coinnich lies in a rough corner of Skye, one of the delectable areas of true wilderness where access is far from easy. The mountain is one of the first aspects of the island seen, but probably not recognised, by visitors arriving via Kyle of Lochalsh. A better view is gained from Glenelg, across the Sound of Sleat.

The pathless ascent from Bealach Udal is unremittingly rough and crag-ridden, but can be eased, slightly, by setting off from a little lower down Kylerhea Glen, from the point where the road starts to descend steeply towards Kylerhea. From here it is possible to reach the south ridge, though it is not very prominent as such, by keeping to the left of a conspicuous buttress (due south of the small lochan at 760209 Ⓐ, which should be the first objective).

Once round the buttress, head for the south ridge and another, larger lochan at 759220 Ⓑ, from where it becomes possible to gain the summit ridge and so the top of the hill. Higher up, much of the difficult terrain is left behind, moving rather more easily on short turf, that comes as a fine reward for the effort lower down.

The summit view is spectacular – a phrase that could be used for almost every mountain top on Skye – embracing the kyles, the mainland peaks, and the great thumb of the Sleat peninsula.

The speediest return is by the outward route, though the ascent of Sgurr na Coinnich is usually combined with that of Beinn na Caillich (see Walk 24) – but that is really one for the toughies, or those who know a good thing when they see it.

Ben Aslak

Start	Bealach Udal, Kylerhea Glen
Distance	3 miles (5km)
Approximate time	2 hours
Parking	Bealach Udal
Refreshments	Broadford, Glenelg
Ordnance Survey maps	Landranger 33 (Loch Alsh, Glen Shiel & Loch Hourn), Explorer 413 (Knoydart, Loch Hourn & Loch Duich)

The comparatively easy summit of Ben Aslak is best tackled from the high point of the Kylerhea Glen, at the Bealach Udal, just to the east of which there is limited parking. At first, the mountain looks formidable, but the ascent proves easier than expected and is well worth it for the excellent panorama it gives.

The sinuous road that leaves the Broadford road for Kylerhea Glen passes through one of the few truly wild places left on Skye. Here, heather moorland, punctuated by rocky outcrops and bogs, plays host to passing buzzards, golden eagles, pipits, skylarks, and not much else. Incredibly, this is the way drovers brought their cattle from the heart of Skye to swim the sound to Glenelg before an onward march to the lowland trysts, or even to London. Slack water was very much a condition of success, as anyone who

Beinn Bheag and Ben Aslak from Kylerhea Glen

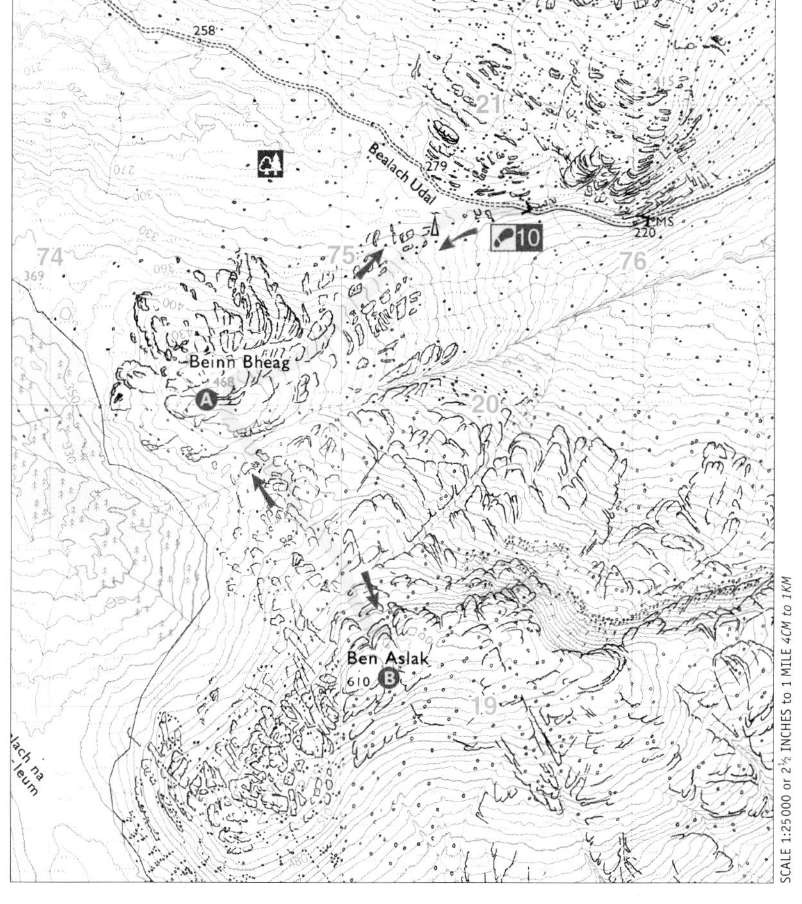

0 200 400 600 800 METRES 1 KILOMETRES
0 200 400 600 YARDS ½ MILES

has watched the tide rip through here like a river in spate, will know.

Above the kyle, Ben Aslak rises to a modest 2000 ft (610m) in height, and therefore by some standards deemed a mountain – one foot less in height and it would be largely ignored.

The approach from Bealach Udal involves 1380 ft (420m) of ascent, and, passing an aerial, first tackles a minor top, Beinn Bheag Ⓐ, reached across heathery, crag-punctuated slopes that in spring and early summer are bright with the yellow eyes of tormentil and the white candy tufts of bog cotton.

Go south and south-east from Beinn Bheag to gain a narrow col, before ascending to a small lochan, and from there pulling up more heathery slopes, aiming slightly closer to south (right) as you approach the summit Ⓑ.

Ben Aslak has a surprise lochan, and two summits about 1300 ft (400m) apart, the higher generally accepted as being that to the west. Both, however, are outstanding viewpoints: the westerly summit for views of the distant Cuillin, while the eastern top gives appetising glimpses into the rough mainland ground of Knoydart beyond Loch Hourn. To the north rise the lumps of Sgurr na Coinnich and Beinn na Caillich.

The only sensible way back is to retrace the outward route.

Broadford coast walk

Start	Broadford
Distance	5 miles (8km)
Approximate time	2½ hours
Parking	Broadford
Refreshments	Broadford
Ordnance Survey maps	Landranger 32 (South Skye & Cuillin Hills), Explorer 412 (Skye – Sleat)

This easy walk occupies the wedge of land north of the A850-Portree road, and north-west of Broadford. Good paths start and finish the walk, though the intervening section is rough and pathless. The final return to Broadford is along what remains of the old narrow road to Portree.

Leave the main Broadford car park (near the tourist information centre) and turn right, heading towards Portree. After the bridge take the first turning on the right, and go down to the pier. Keep ahead through a gate, following the on-going road past Corry Lodge to reach the shore path at an iron gate.

Memorial, Broadford

Shortly, climb left to the top of a low headland, Rubh' an Eireannaich (Irishman's Point) **A**. Cross a fence and go round the corner of a wall to follow the path through autumn's heather back to the shore, with fine views of the far mainland, and the more local islands – the Crowlins, Pabay, Longay, Scalpay and Guillamon Island – for company.

When another fence is crossed (stile) **B**, rougher walking begins, switching between the basaltic rocks of the shore and heather knolls above. *Care is needed on basalt, but especially if it is wet.* There is no path, so take it easy: this is a place to relax and linger, and agreeably attractive in early summer when the wild flowers are at their best. With the sort of perversity that some walkers will appreciate, this is also an enjoyable walk in the teeth of a Skye storm when progress is an exhilarating, breath-taking push against the elements.

Eventually, the route rejoins the shore near a clearing **C**, once occupied by

Man, as the remains of croft buildings testify. The difficult going now eases and passes onto a path between woodland and the shore. At a bend, a small bay comes into view, leading on to Rubha na Sgianadin. Dominating the view, Beinn na Caillich, the hill of the old woman, is a huge scree dome topped by a massive cairn. Beneath the cairn, it is said, lies a Norwegian princess. When the princess lay dying, and knew that the end of her life was imminent, she asked that she might be buried, as Seton Gordon recounts in *The Charm of Skye*, 'full in the track of the Black Wind that sweeps, pure, cold, and vital, across from the shores of Lochlin, hundreds of leagues beneath the pale northern horizon.' Over her body, her compatriots erected a huge cairn, while beneath her body, so the story goes, lies a casket of gold.

Amble around Camas Sgianadin **D**, a pleasant bay, and then join a forest trail back to the main road, reaching the A850 near the cemetery.

All that remains is to follow the old road back to Broadford. ●

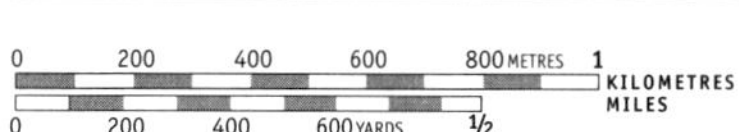

SCALE 1:25 000 or 2½ INCHES to 1 MILE *4CM to 1KM*

Acairseid an Rubha

Start	Aird of Sleat
Distance	3½ miles (5.8km)
Approximate time	2 hours
Parking	Road end, Aird of Sleat
Refreshments	Armadale
Ordnance Survey maps	Landranger 32 (South Skye & Cuillin Hills), Explorer 412 (Skye – Sleat)

This short, but not-to-be-underestimated, expedition to the southern end of Skye crams many delights into the journey, especially in spring and early summer when the fields are ablaze with colour. The objective is the narrow inlet of Acairseid an Rubha, which offers a surprise view of the Cuillin and though some visitors want to press on to the southernmost tip of Skye, at the lighthouse, this is not really a feasible option for casual walkers: the path is virtually non-existent, the terrain at its most arduous (and boggy) with no easy variants, and the exact whereabouts of the lighthouse a mystery until near the very end.

The approach is along the road from Ardvasar to the Aird of Sleat, where parking is very limited and needs to be accomplished with consideration for others.

The name Sleat (pronounced slate) derives from *sleibhte*, meaning an extensive tract of moorland, and so it is. This appropriately named thumb of rugged, lochan-laden moorland, crumples into a thousand nooks and crannies where Man has battled with the elements to win a living from the unforgiving land. Yet, ironically, Sleat is regarded as 'The Garden of Skye', though not without dissent, for to some extent the gardens are the product of an unhappy time in the island's history,

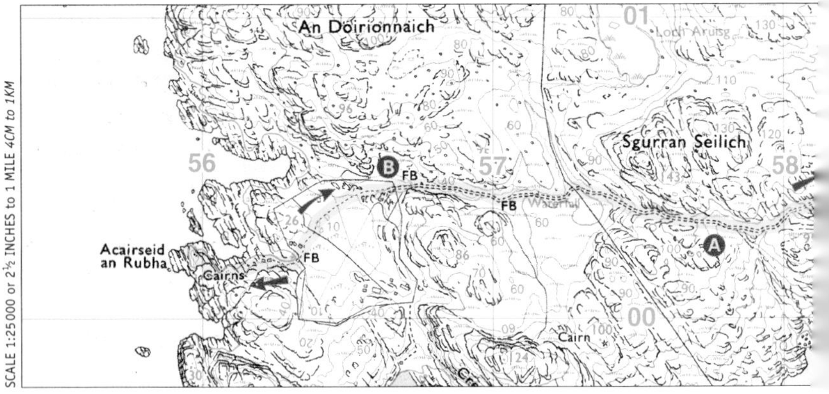

when clan chieftains succumbed to the rule of London, and rode roughshod over the lives and necessities of their tenants. This is nowhere better exemplified than along the tortuous but delightful looping road that visits the isolated communities at Ord, Tokavaig and Tarskavaig, founded at the time of the notorious Highland Clearances when people were forcibly removed from better ground to make way for sheep, and found themselves clinging, almost literally, to the edges of the land.

The concept of an island garden comes, too, from Sleat's more sheltered environment, that allows beech, sycamore and alien conifers to flourish alongside the more natural birch, alder and bramble.

The walk begins through a gate at the road head, and along a broad, rough track that climbs steadily to provide a fine view of the island of Eigg and the shapely Cuillin of Rum. More undulations through a rocky, hummocky landscape climb to the highest point of the track, a small bealach Ⓐ, or pass, from where the onward route wanders downwards towards a distant bay. Initially steep, the descent then leads across a wide hollow through which flows a burn

The bay at Acairseid an Rubha

issuing from nearby Loch Aruisg, making a modest splash of a small waterfall and pool before meandering onwards through a rocky gorge.

Go to a gate (ignoring a tempting path with a tiny sign suggesting a route to the lighthouse and a sandy beach – this is quite arduous and not part of this walk), and immediately after this, when the track forks Ⓑ, bear right along a path that leads to a white cottage at the edge of the narrow harbour. A gate at the top end of the inlet gives onto a slab bridge and a path leading right, passing another cottage, to the sea and a surprise view of the Cuillin. Off-shore, the Cuillin of Rum make an equally daunting spectacle.

Along the route, derelict buildings and lush growths of fuchsia, tell of a more substantial community here than the two crofts that are occupied now. At one time, this tiny fishing harbour supported a population of 80, though the land is intolerant and slow to yield anything other than bog myrtle, heather, ragwort and bog cotton. Even so, there is a need to respect privacy and property here: the cottages are not derelict, and are occupied; the crofts are worked. Please do not disturb the people who live here.

The return simply retraces the outward route.

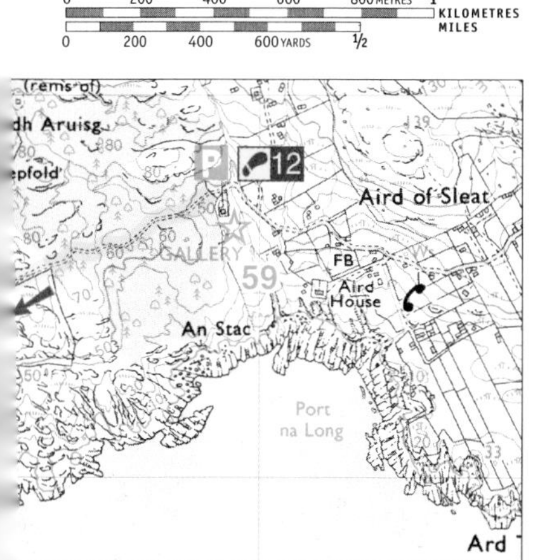

Camasunary

Start	Kilmarie
Distance	5 miles (8km)
Approximate time	2½ hours (plus time at Camasunary)
Parking	Kilmarie
Refreshments	Elgol or Torrin (seasonal), Broadford
Ordnance Survey maps	Landranger 32 (South Skye & Cuillin Hills), Explorer 411 (Skye – Cuillin Hills)

There can be no more idyllic spot on Skye for peace and tranquillity than the lovely bay of Camasunary, or Camas Fhionnairigh to give it its Gaelic form. Lazy waves lap on a pebbly shore backed by the crags of Sgurr na Stri and great swards of green grass overlie all sorts of colourful rubble that pokes through the surface like alien plant life. This walk from Kilmarie is the most direct and easiest way of reaching Camasunary, though strong walkers can complete Walk 18 from Sligachan, all the way through the glen.

For one of the most dramatic surprise views on Skye, it is difficult to better that from Am Màm, the broad bealach due east of the bay of Camasunary. Whether the subsequent descent to Camasunary is undertaken is largely irrelevant, but the bay is a splendid retreat from daily life.

At the roadside at Kilmarie, a plaque announces that the track to Camasunary was constructed in 1968 by army engineers. Sadly, this plan was less altruistic than might be supposed, the work being intended to enable improvements to be made to the route around the coastline from Camasunary to Loch Coruisk, to make access easier for anglers. This would have meant the destruction of the alarming feature known as the Bad Step, a steep and unavoidable slab of rock directly above the sea. The climbing world objected, and the Bad Step survived, which is more than can be said for the bridge that once spanned the tidal Abhainn Camas Fhionnairigh; it was taken down in the 1980s, and now only rusted stanchions remain.

The route to Am Màm is clear throughout, and the hillsides either side often patrolled by golden eagles. A broad track begins from the gate opposite the parking space. Am Màm is the low col directly ahead, over which the tops of the highest Cuillin summit poke tantalisingly.

Crossing a couple of minor fords en route the stony track climbs to a cairn marking the top of the pass **A**, opening up a stunning view. To the right is Bla Bheinn's south ridge and the dark pinnacles of the Black Cuillin across Srath na Crèitheach. Directly below, the green coastal pastures hug the sandy beach backed by the rugged profile of Sgurr na Stri. Seaward, across Loch

The bothy at Camasunary

Scavaig, the pinnacled island of Rum sails across the horizon beyond the low-lying hour-glass shape of Soay, used in the 1940s as a base for a shark fishing industry by Gavin Maxwell. This is a magnificent setting, and time spent here is time well spent.

A short way across the bealach, the descent to Camasunary begins, zigzagging down easily. Shortcuts on the way down do nothing other than nominally hasten progress. Of the two buildings at Camasunary, the far one is an open bothy, and an ideal base from which those who don't mind roughing it a bit can explore the area.

The return trip simply follows the outward route, the climb to Am Màm yielding more easily than might be expected.

Alternative finish: For those who can cope with airy, clifftop walking on a rugged, narrow and frequently wet path, there is an alternative way out from Camasunary, which involves following the coastline as far as Elgol. This is 3¾ miles (6km) long, and, if transport hasn't been arranged, with a good chunk of road walking needed to get back to Kilmarie.

Walk away from the buildings at Camasunary, on a path that leads directly to a crossing of the Abhainn nan Leac at a ford Ⓑ, beyond which the on-going path runs across a boggy stretch of ground to start climbing above the sea cliffs. If the burn is in spate, follow the track up to the bridge used on the descent into Camasunary, from there returning along the course of the burn to locate the path.

The path improves as it climbs above Rubha na h-Airighe Bàine, a low cliff that sports an assortment of trees – silver birch, goat willow, hazel, ash, holly and the occasional white poplar. With a couple of awkward steps down, the path eventually runs on to descend steeply through bracken to a spread of iris at Cladach a'Ghlinne, the entrance to Glen Scaladal Ⓒ. (*NOTE: In an emergency Glen Scaladal can be used as an escape route back to Kilmarie.*)

Ford the burn issuing from Glen Scaladal, and locate the on-going path as it rises to tackle to cliffs below Ben Cleat. What follows is another helping of superb clifftop walking. The path is continuous throughout, but wet and slippery in places. As it reaches the

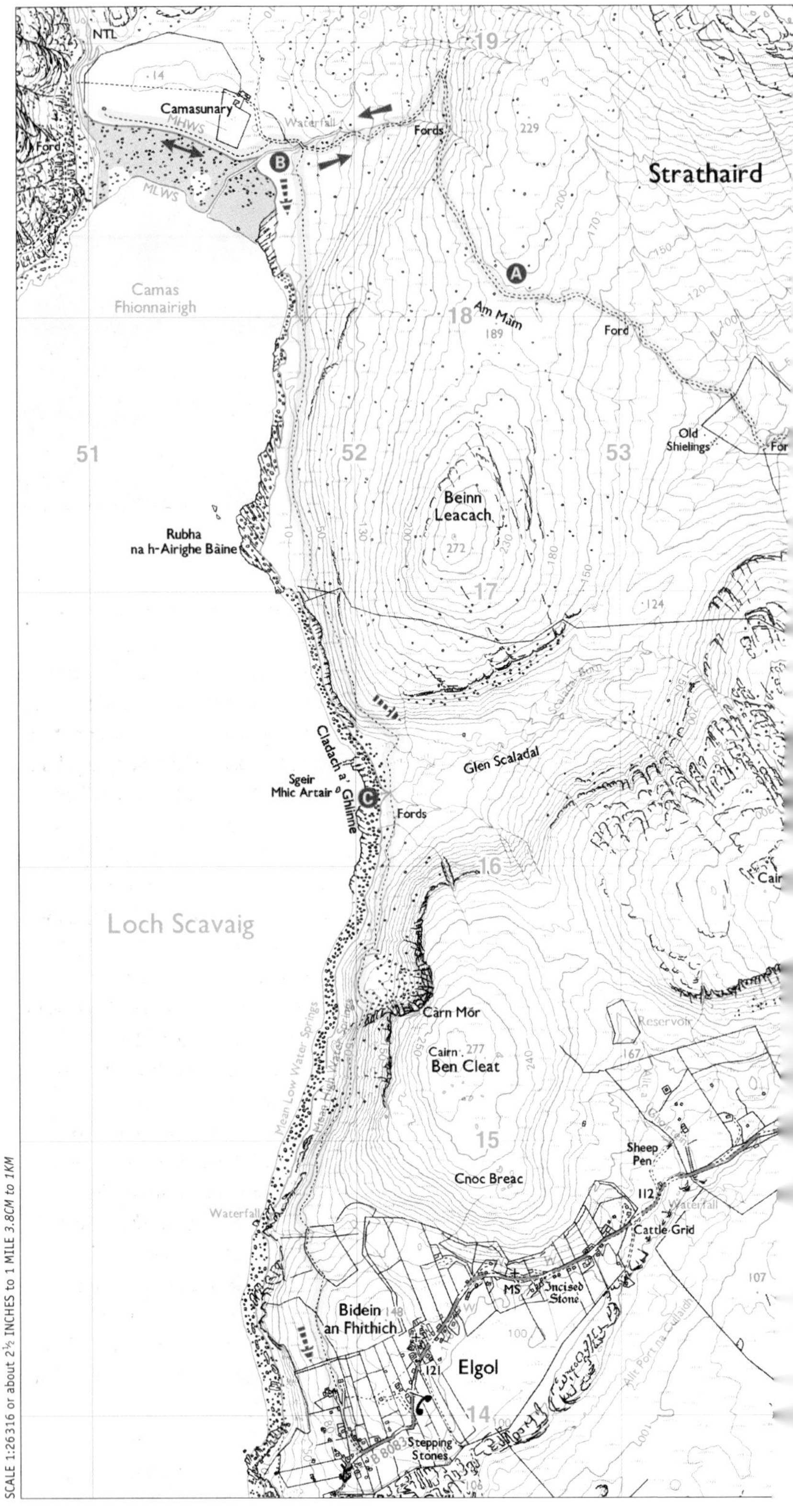

SCALE 1:26316 or about 2½ INCHES to 1 MILE 3.8CM to 1KM

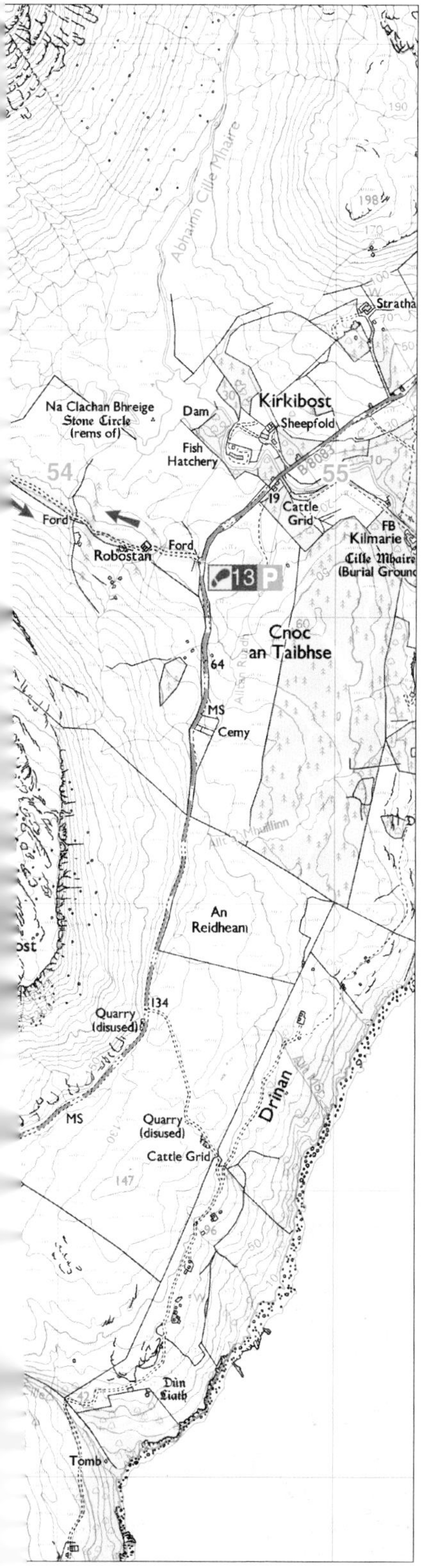

Pebble beach at Camasunary

boundary fence of Elgol, climb steeply upwards beside the fence for a short distance to a gate, from which a track runs, right, to reach the road. If heading for Elgol's bouldery shore, turn right. If returning by road to Kilmarie, turn left.

Linked to Broadford by a post bus service that runs twice daily, Elgol is very much the end of the road, lying almost at the tip of the Strathaird peninsula. Best known for its dramatic, if distant, views of the Cuillin, Elgol is the setting off point for boat trips to Loch Coruisk, and the point of access to the cave in which Prince Charles Edward Stuart (Bonnie Prince Charlie) spent his last night on Skye.

According to tradition, Vortigern despatched his lieutenant Aella and five ships to explore the Western Isles. Resistant to 'exploration' the people of Skye raised what ships they could and intercepted Aella at the entrance to Loch Scavaig and engaged him in battle. Aella's ships were driven off, but his name remains enshrined in the first syllable of Elgol. ●

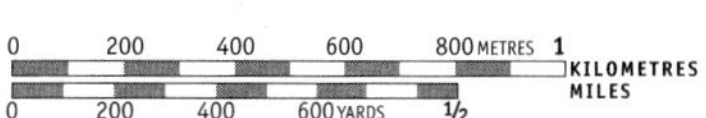

Loch Achaidh na h-Inich

Start	Balmacara Square
Distance	5 miles (8km)
Approximate time	2–3 hours
Parking	Balmacara Square
Refreshments	Balmacara Square
Ordnance Survey maps	Landrangers 24 (Raasay, Applecross & Loch Torridon) and 33 (Loch Alsh, Glen Shiel & Loch Hourn) Explorer 428 (Kyle of Lochalsh, Plockton & Applecross)

This delightful introduction to the National Trust for Scotland's Balmacara Estate features the splendid sprawl of Coille Mhór, the big wood, the largest area of native birch and willow woodland on the estate, and understandably a Site of Special Scientific Interest. The objective of the walk is the glorious spread of Loch Achaidh na h-Inich (pronounced Achna-hee-nee). The return journey is by the same route (unless transport can be arranged), but this walk will combine easily with Walk 15 over Duncraig Hill to give a longer excursion of 10¼ miles (16.5km).

Balmacara Estate comprises eight townships including the conservation village of Plockton. Crofting – traditional small-scale farming – has been carried out on the estate for more than 200 years, and this has shaped the settlements seen today and the varied landscape of the estate. Crofting was widespread throughout the Scottish Highlands until the period known as the 'Highland Clearances' (late 18th, early 19th centuries), during which many tenants and their families were brutally evicted to permit the introduction of sheep farming. The displaced crofters often moved to inhospitable ground near the coast and on the islands, though many of the communities that were so formed were eventually abandoned, and contributed to the depopulation of the Highlands.

Ruined building near Loch Achaidh na h-Inich

From the parking area, walk to the right of the village green and duck pond and then up the rising lane ahead. On approaching a large house near the top of the ascent, leave the road by turning onto a track, through a gate, signposted to Achnahinich. The track climbs gently before descending to a ford Ⓐ, after which a kissing-gate and stile give onto a path that soon crosses a small area of open ground where in summer wild flowers grow in profusion.

The path soon enters the confines of Coille Mhór where the trees boast a splendid display of lichen and bracket fungus. Cross a small stream, and continue climbing beyond to pass the distinctive rocky cone of Sgurr Beag.

Towards the top edge of the woodland there is a fine retrospective view to Balmacara and out across Loch Alsh. To the left is the craggy shape of Sgurr Mor, while farther afield, the hills of Skye put in an appearance.

Eventually, the path breaks free of the woodland, and runs on across heather moorland Ⓑ, aiming initially for the masted Duncraig Hill, and then suddenly Loch Achaidh na h-Inich slips into view. The path turns once more into birch and willow woodland, wandering down to pass a ruined enclosure, and finally emerges at a signpost a few strides from the edge of Loch Achaidh na h-Inich.

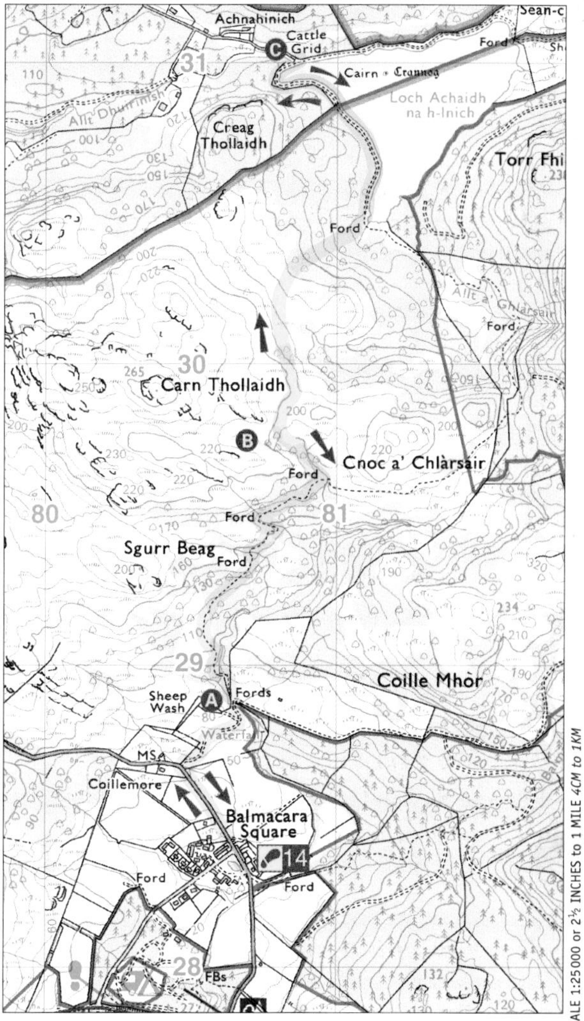

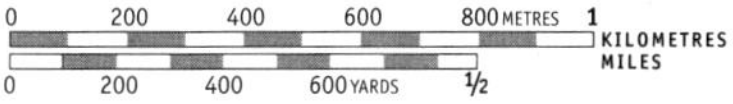

Turn left and follow the water's edge path as far as a gate, with lovely views over the lily-rimmed, reedy loch along the way. Beyond the gate the on-going track is muddy after wet weather, *so anyone visiting only Loch Achaidh na h-Inich will find this a convenient place to turn round.* Otherwise, continue past the gate and follow a track out to meet a surfaced road Ⓒ, where this walk meets Walk 15. This is a peaceful place to perch and admire the loch, the edge of Eden. Within the loch lie the remains of a crannog, a man-made island.

When the time comes to return, simply retrace the track to the gate, and then the water's-edge path to the signpost, before climbing through birch, willow and bracken on the outward route. The way back is every bit as delightful as the way out.

SCALE 1:25 000 or $2\frac{1}{2}$ INCHES to 1 MILE 4CM to 1KM

0 200 400 600 800 METRES 1 KILOMETRES
0 200 400 600 YARDS ½ MILES

Duncraig Hill (Carn a'Bhealach Mhoir)

Start	Achnandarach
Distance	5¼ miles (8.5km)
Approximate time	2–3 hours
Parking	Achnandarach
Refreshments	Plockton, Kyle of Lochalsh
Ordnance Survey maps	Landranger 24 (Raasay, Applecross & Loch Torridon), Explorer 428 (Kyle of Lochalsh, Plockton & Applecross)

In spite of radar masts that bedevil its summit, Duncraig Hill is a rewarding objective, reached, in this walk, by a circular route from the straggling hamlet of Achnandarach. Part of the walk, which visits reedy lochans, dense pine plantations and rocky summits, uses quiet roads, with the rest on forest tracks and stony trails. Walkers who want a slightly longer day can combine this easily with Walk 14, starting at Balmacara Square and heading for Loch Achaidh na h-Inich first. This would produce a walk of 10¼ miles (16.5km).

From the parking area at Achnandarach turn right and walk to a road junction. Just before the junction, keep an eye open for the bright yellow monkeyflower, a plant that was introduced into Britain from Unalaska Island (off the coast of Alaska) in the early 19th century, but which soon escaped from gardens and now colonises wet places throughout Britain.

At the road junction, turn right, walking alongside a dense plantation, and soon passing Loch Lundie. Beyond the end of the loch the road starts to descend, having freed itself from the plantation.

Just before the descending road bends distinctly left, leave it by branching right to a gate and onto an old track that heads into Creagdaroch Wood Ⓐ. The track rises steadily and goes past a signposted turning for Duncraig. Keep forward to a cattle grid, where the track leaves the plantation. Off to the left, a clear view appears towards the mouth of Loch Carron. Above, the crags of Duncraig Hill seem impassable, but continue with the on-going track as far as a turning on the left Ⓑ, a service road that leads up to the relay masts on the summit of the hill.

Turn onto the track and follow it through the plantation, then climb into a rocky gorge, passing a large metal deer gate. The gorge proves to be the key to the ascent of Duncraig Hill – its proper name is Carn a'Bhealach Mhoir, after the 'big pass' at the top of the gorge. The view eastwards is one of rocky, lochy hummocks and hollows, impressive, but not for idle wandering.

Follow the broad track to the summit of Duncraig Hill. Near the masts a large boulder is topped by a cairn, though there is clearly higher ground to the north. Try hard to ignore the masts, admiring instead the extensive panorama north to Applecross, Torridon and Strathcarron, south to Beinn Sgritheall, sentinel of Knoydart, and then virtually the whole of the Skye mountains, and the flat-topped peak of Dun Caan on Raasay.

Go back down the service road to rejoin the original line, and there turn left **B**, soon reaching another deer gate and re-entering the plantation. The track comes down to intercept a broad forest trail. Cross this and maintain the same direction to emerge from the plantation at another gate, near the turning for Achnahinich Farm **C**.

Keep forward, and soon walk along the edge of lovely Loch Achaidh na h-Inich, in the middle of which stand the remains of a crannog. This is a man-made island of a type first noted in prehistoric times but used fairly extensively in later times. They were made by driving piles of timber into the lake bed and then filling them with boulders, and they were often approached by a causeway sunk just below the surface of the water so that invaders would have difficulty finding the way to the island. The one in Loch Achaidh na h-Inich was occupied until the 17th century.

Continue alongside the loch to a signposted path on the left, for Balmacara **D** – *which would be the turning point for anyone who started in Balmacara.* Here, keep ahead over a cattle grid, soon reaching the straggling cottages at Achnandarach. The road then descends beside a moss-covered wall at the edge of a dense plantation and shortly returns to the starting point. ●

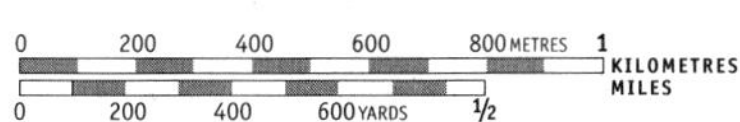

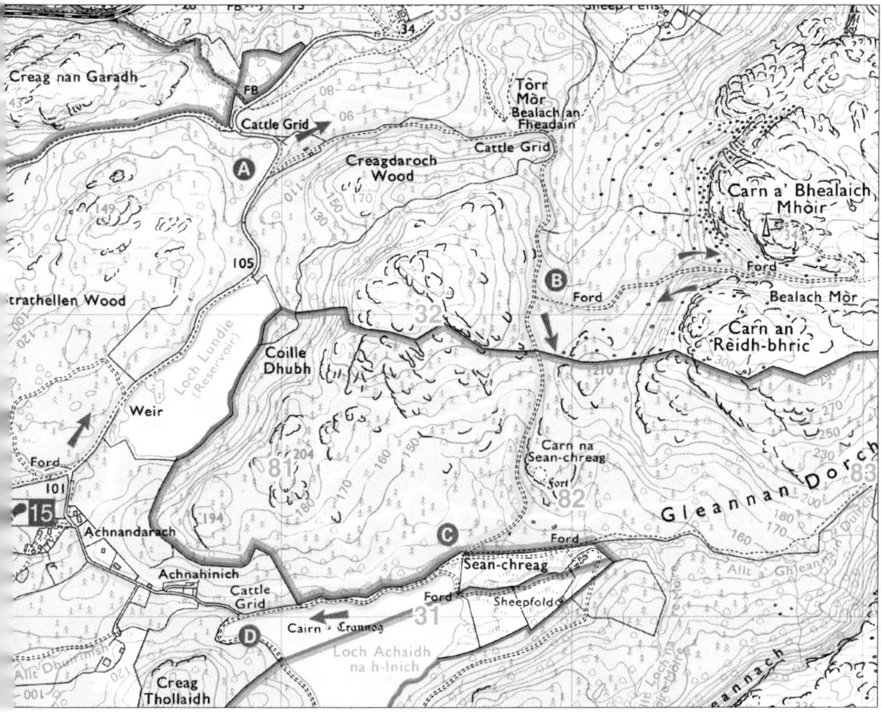

SCALE 1:25 000 or 2½ INCHES to 1 MILE *4CM to 1KM*

Sgurr an Airgid

Start	Clachan Duich, Morvich
Distance	6¼ miles (10km)
Approximate time	3–4 hours
Parking	Clachan Duich
Refreshments	Shiel Bridge, Dornie
Ordnance Survey maps	Landranger 33 (Loch Alsh, Glen Shiel & Loch Hourn), Explorer 413 (Knoydart, Loch Hourn & Loch Duich)

This magnificent viewpoint only succumbs to a determined assault, but the reward is amazing. It is not clear how the mountain came to be named Sgurr an Airgid (pronounced Errakit), the Silver Peak. Some have suggested that it was because of the way sunlight reflects off its rocks and myriad streams. The mountain presents its best side to the east, and has an enticing profile when seen from Gleann Lichd, for example.

The best place to start is from the cemetery at Clachan Duich, and from there walk along the road as far as a barely noticeable bridge (solitary tree nearby) just *after* a rough turning to corrugated iron-roofed agricultural buildings and *before* the turning for the Falls of Glomach car park Ⓐ.

From the bridge take an indistinct path along the true left bank of a small burn until this intercepts a more evident path, heading steeply left through bracken and across the hill slope. The path shortly angles back to reach a gate in a deer fence Ⓑ. Go through the gate in the fence and stick with the path as it

Sgurr an Airgid from Strath Croe

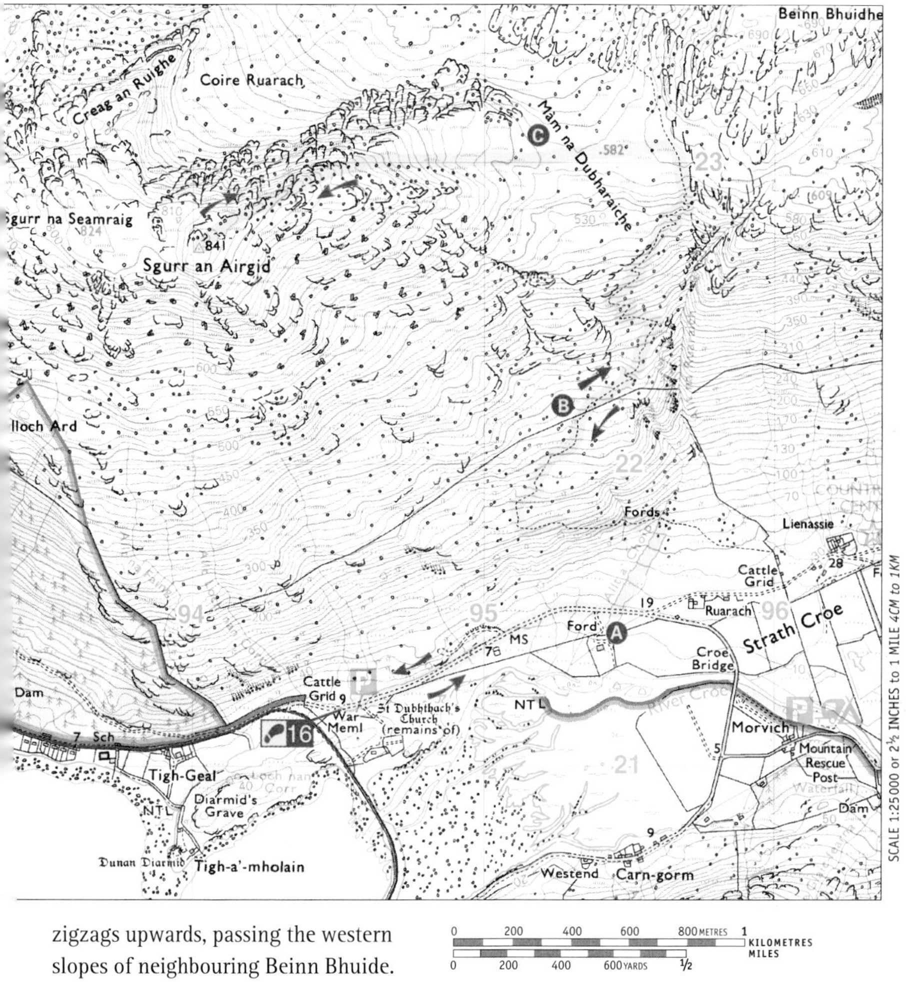

SCALE 1:25000 or 2½ INCHES to 1 MILE 4CM to 1KM

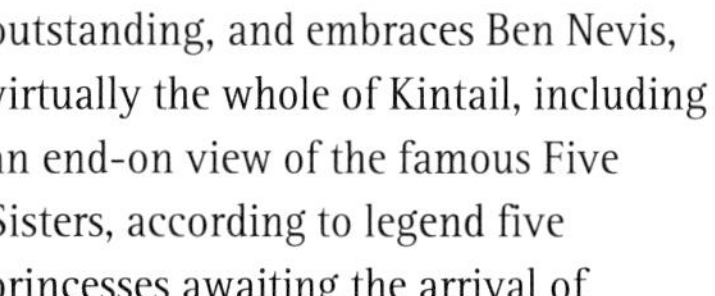

zigzags upwards, passing the western slopes of neighbouring Beinn Bhuide. Higher up, the path seems to lose the plot and all but disappears, but by then this is unimportant. Off to the left, on approaching the top of the climb, a green cove **C** between rocky outcrops provides an easy approach to the summit, although the rocky ribs are easy enough. It is wise counsel to make a mental note of the whereabouts of the top of the ascent path to avoid unwanted and potentially difficult casting about on the way down.

The summit is marked by a triangulation pillar, but the view suddenly and dramatically illustrates why the effort of getting here was so worthwhile. The panorama is outstanding, and embraces Ben Nevis, virtually the whole of Kintail, including an end-on view of the famous Five Sisters, according to legend five princesses awaiting the arrival of promised princes. The view takes in much of Skye, Rum, Eigg, and the vast sweep of Applecross and Torridon. Close by, the scenery is a confused and delightfully contorted display of hummocks, hollows and lochans.

The only way down is the way of ascent; *no attempt should be made to shorten the descent, any other possibility is imagined and dangerous, leading to steep rock and grass slopes.*

Bla Bheinn

Start	Loch Slapin
Distance	5 miles (8km)
Approximate time	4–5 hours
Parking	Near bridge over Allt na Dunaiche, ½ mile (1km) beyond the head of Loch Slapin.
Refreshments	Torrin and Elgo (seasonal), Broadford
Ordnance Survey maps	Landranger 32 (South Skye & Cuillin Hills), Explorer 411 (Skye – Cuillin Hills)

The thoughtfulness of Jethro Tull band member Ian Anderson, who owned Bla Bheinn, in agreeing to sell at a generous price, meant that it could be bought by the John Muir Trust, an organisation dedicated to safeguarding and protecting Scotland's wilder landscapes. Bla Bheinn is the highest and most southerly of the Cuillin Outliers, and links with the westernmost Red Cuillin in a continuous chain of hills from the southern tip of Strathaird to Sligachan. The customary ascent is by the east ridge, even though, viewed end on, this looks impossibly steep. This is not a walk for other than clear and settled conditions.

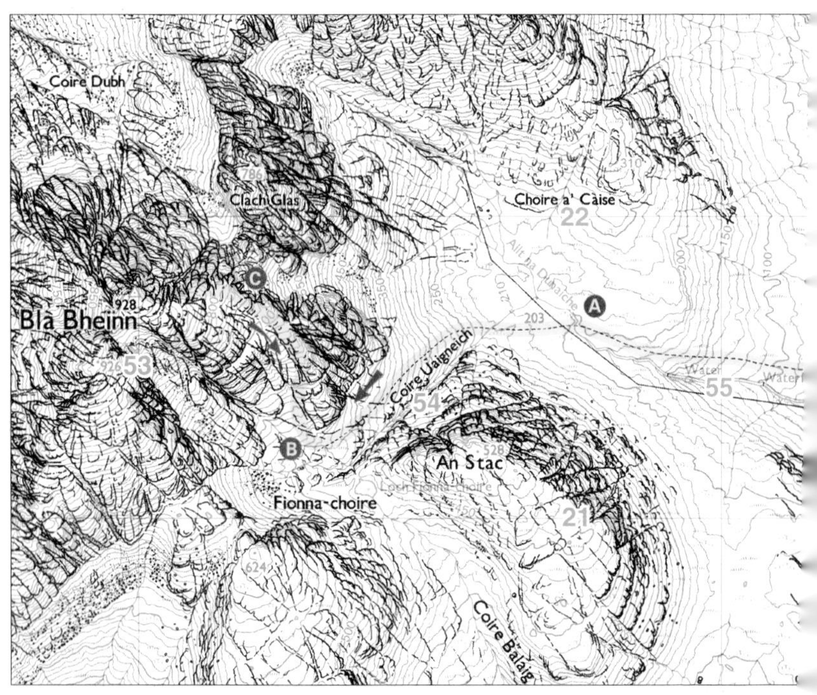

Post bus: a useful way of reaching the start of the ascent to Bla Bheinn

The relatively short distance involved in climbing Bla Bheinn is meaningless. As the walk starts almost at sea level, it follows that there is a lot of uphill work to be done (3000 ft/915m, in fact), and much of it on rock.

From the car park provided by the John Muir Trust, follow the good path that runs along the north bank of the Allt na Dunaiche, weaving through a wooded gorge and around heathery hummocks, and passing some fine waterfalls en route.

The Allt na Dunaiche is variously called the 'Burn of Sorrow', or the 'Burn of Misfortune', a name that alludes to the story of seven girls and a young boy who went to spend the summer in a shieling up above the waterfall, where the burn rises. One day, the girls went out to a wedding, leaving the boy alone. During his lonely vigil, the shieling was entered by seven large cats, who seated themselves by the fire, and talked. The boy watched, spellbound. Then the cats arose, took all the goodness from the butter and the cream, leaving but the appearance of goodness, and vanished. When the girls came home, and the terrified child recounted the story, the girls, seeing what appeared to be butter and cream in plenty, laughed at him, saying it was a dream. Next night, back came the cats, and by dawn all the girls were dead. Later that day, when their mothers came to fetch the butter and cream, as was customary, each, as they entered the shieling and saw the dead girls, cried out 'Airidh mo dunach' (the Shieling of Misfortune).

Farther on, cross the Allt na Dunaiche (A), beyond which the path starts tending to the left to reach a tributary stream at the foot of Coire Uaigneich. A mix of grass and loose stone lies ahead, now ascending more strenuously to pass a large buttress that forms the end of the east ridge. Soon the upper part of the corrie is reached, with Loch Fionna-choire and the satellite, An Stac, off to the east, and the Great Scree Gully directly above (B). For much of the

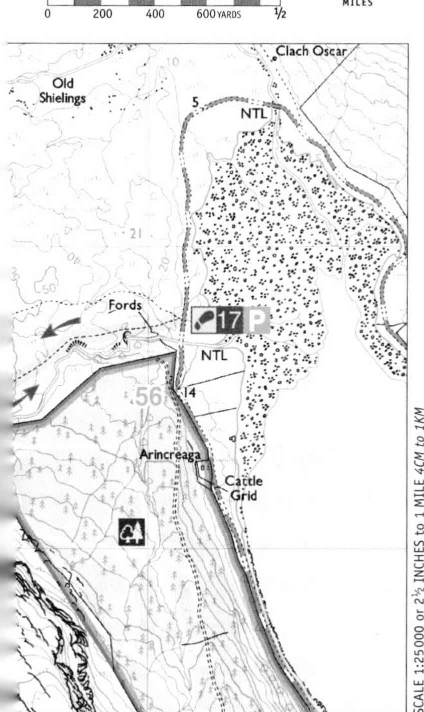

way the path is clear and cairned, though once the upper corrie is reached, both become less obvious.

Now swing round to the right and tackle steep grass and rocks to gain the east ridge. There are a number of possible lines, all reaching the broad crest of the ridge at some point; once this is achieved, the onward route is much more evident, and ascends through stony grooves and up rocky buttresses to a spectacular view of Clach Glas between the walls of an intervening gully Ⓒ.

Continue ascending, with more views of Clach Glas, before progressing upwards on a clearly-trodden path with a little (avoidable) easy scrambling en route, before finally emerging on the summit shoulder, with only a short, easy walk up to the trigangulation point and cairn remaining. The view of the Cuillin that greets the last few strides is breathtaking and sudden, and matched only by that of the great gullies sweeping down into Glen Sligachan.

To return, retrace the ascent, though this may prove difficult and potentially dangerous in misty conditions. *If mists do suddenly appear, head for the col between the two summits and descend the Great Scree Gully, with the greatest care.* ●

Heading to Bla Bheinn

Glen Sligachan

Start	Sligachan
Distance	7¾ miles (12.5km)
Approximate time	4–5 hours
Parking	Sligachan
Refreshments	Sligachan
Ordnance Survey maps	Landranger 32 (South Skye & Cuillin Hills), Explorer 411 (Skye – Cuillin Hills)

This stunning glen, the finest on Skye, forms the eastern boundary of Minginish, separating the Cuillin from Strathaird. For walkers it is an ideal place to become familiar with Skye terrain, and the sort of difficulties it presents. The complete walk from Sligachan to Camasunary is for anyone a magnificent proposition, but the distances through the glen should not be underestimated, and the going can at times be very trying. Anyone in search of a long low-level walk will find nothing better on Skye. The route given here presupposes that the walker will either return to Sligachan (quite a day, doubling the distance given) or arrange a pickup at Kilmarie.

Progress through Glen Sligachan is invariably affected by the recent weather. After heavy or sustained rain, expect to ford many of the burns (or make tiring detours) and to plod through what seems like an eight-mile long bog. Yet in good conditions, it can be so remarkably different. The walking, nevertheless, ranks as magnificent in any conditions. Walkers unable to arrange pickups or to complete the whole walk should consider going as far as the Lochan Dubha, near the entrance to Harta Corrie. This in itself is an excellent walk, and presents both Sgurr nan Gillean and Marsco from unfamiliar angles, as well as giving an insight into the depths of Harta Corrie and across to the heights of the Cuillin.

The prominent Clach na Craoibhe Chaoruinn on the way through Glen Sligachan

A Just beyond the old bridge at Sligachan, take the signposted path through a gate for Loch Coruisk. The path moves on in stages: first a long moorland stretch as the route heads towards shapely Marsco, then a stretch dominated by Sgurr nan Gillean. A narrowing follows, as the glen passes the Lochan Dubha and heads for Bla Bheinn before finally bursting out into the loveliness that is Camasunary.

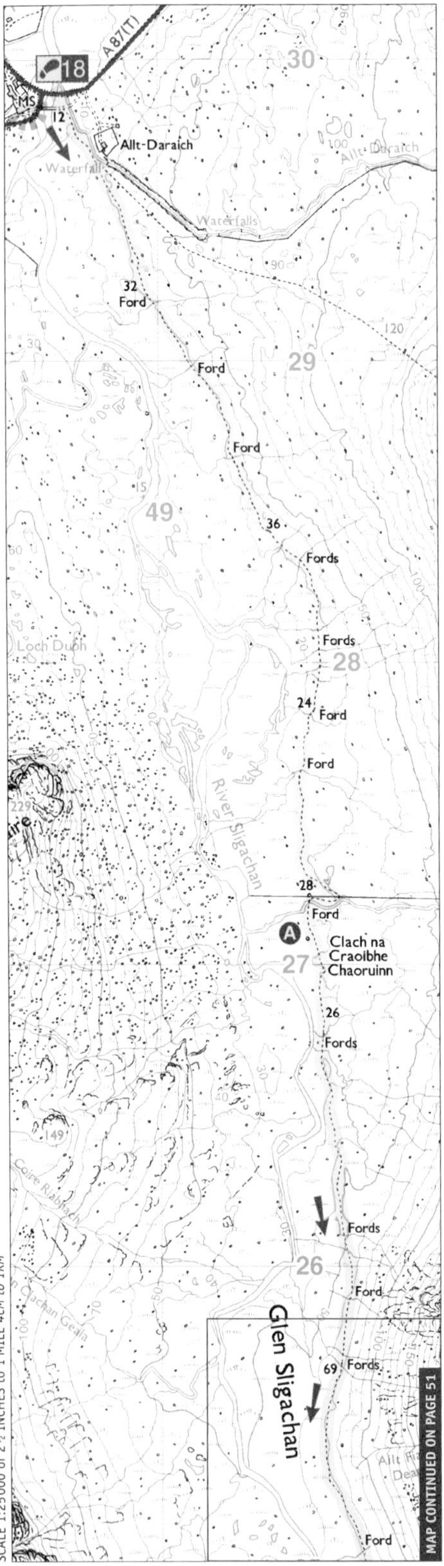

The way encounters numerous feeder burns before reaching the rather more substantial Allt na Measarroch. Cross the burn, almost always a wet proposition, and continue to a prominent heather-topped boulder, Clach na Craoibhe Chaoruinn Ⓐ.

More pleasant walking beneath the great slopes of Marsco ensues, climbing gently to a high point Ⓑ overlooking the Lochan Dubha from where there is a fine view through Harta Corrie to the dark central peaks of the Black Cuillin – Sgurr Alasdair, Sgurr Mhic Choinnich and Sgurr Dearg and its Inaccessible Pinnacle.

At the entrance to the corrie stands a shrub-encrusted boulder, the Bloody Stone, that features among the many tales of the clashes between the MacDonalds and the MacLeods. In 1395 the MacDonalds sent a force of galleys to invade Skye. They landed at Loch Eynort and rapidly progressed east towards Sligachan, where they met a formidable response from the MacLeods, and a furious battle ensued during which the invaders were thrown into confusion, which soon became a rout. The MacLeods ruthlessly pursued them back to Loch Eynort where, with cruel fate, the MacAskills had seized their galleys and moored them off-shore. It is said that not one of the invaders survived, and that the heads of the slain were collected, numbered and

SCALE 1:25 000 or 2½ INCHES to 1 MILE 4CM to 1KM

MAP CONTINUED ON PAGE 51

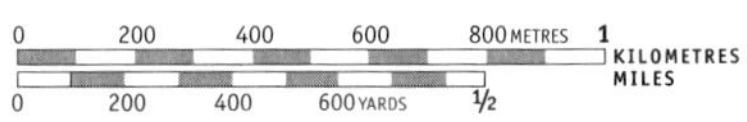

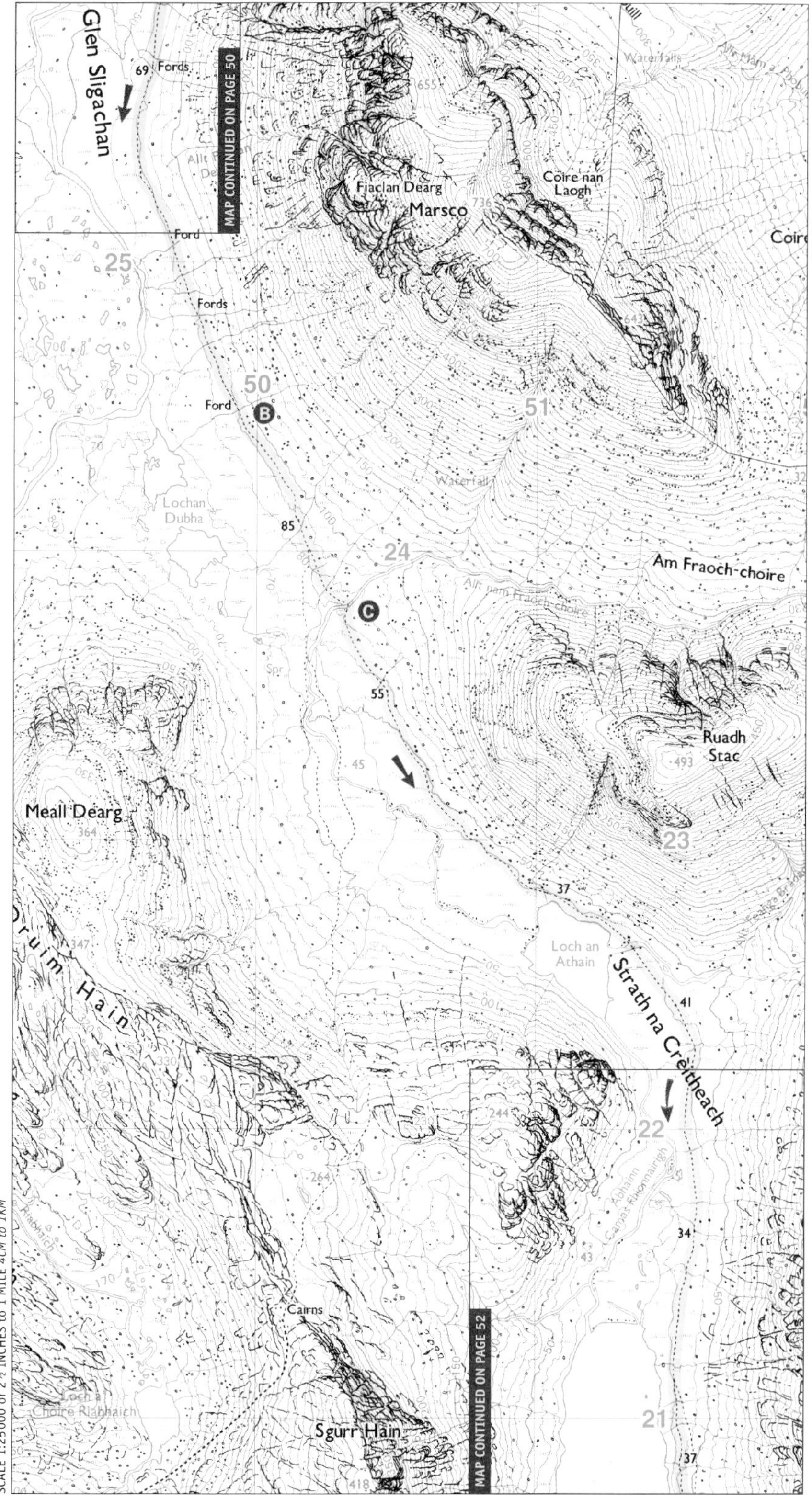
Glen Sligachan
Fords
Ford
Fords
Ford
MAP CONTINUED ON PAGE 50
Fiaclan Dearg
Marsco
736
655
Coire nan Laogh
Waterfalls
Coire
643
Waterfall
Lochan Dubha
Am Fraoch-choire
Allt nam Fraoch-choire
Ruadh Stac
493
Meall Dearg
364
Druim Hain
Loch an Athain
Strath na Creitheach
Abhainn Camas Fhionnairigh
Cairns
Loch a' Choire Riabhaich
Sgurr Hain
418
MAP CONTINUED ON PAGE 52
SCALE 1:25000 or 2½ INCHES to 1 MILE 4CM to 1KM

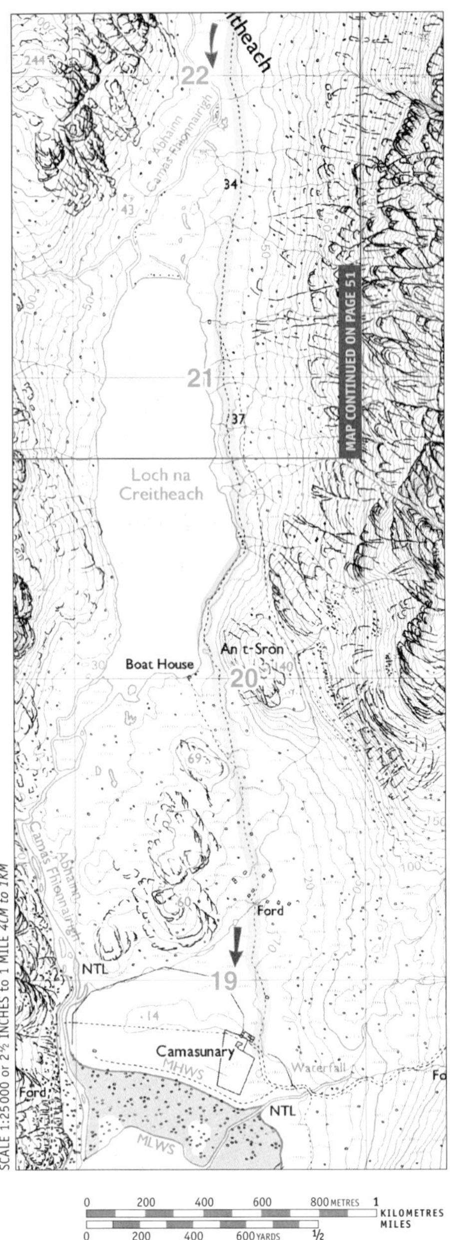

The Pinnacle Ridge of Sgurr nan Gillean, seen from Glen Sligachan

sent to Dunvegan as trophies to be retained in the custody of the warden of Dunvegan Castle. It was at Creag an Fheannaidh, The Rock of the Flaying, now known as the Bloody Stone, that the spoils of battle were divided.

Not far past the two Lochan Dubha, and at the entrance to Am Fraoch-choire, the track forks **C**. The right fork heads for Druim Hain and Loch Coruisk, while the continuation of the glen route runs on first to Loch an Athain and into the dramatic Srath na Crèitheach.

Beneath the long south ridge of Bla Bheinn, the path passes close by Loch na Crèitheach before pressing on to reach Camas Fhionnairigh (anglicised to Camasunary), one of the most enchanting places on the entire island, and an entirely relaxing place to be. Here a wide sandy beach runs into a bright green sward of meadow on which two buildings, one a bothy, the other private, provide a stark contrast to the background darkness of Sgurr na Stri and Bla Bheinn.

To the east, a broad track can be seen slanting up and across the hillside to a low bealach, Am Màm, and this option, rough underfoot but a broad track all the way, leads out to the Elgol-Broadford road at Kilmarie, adding $2\frac{1}{2}$ miles (4km) to the route.

Loch Alsh

Start	Glenelg ferry
Distance	7¾ miles (12.5km)
Approximate time	4–5 hours
Parking	Glenelg ferry
Refreshments	Glenelg
Ordnance Survey maps	Landranger 33 (Loch Alsh, Glen Shiel & Loch Hourn), Explorer 413 (Knoydart, Loch Hourn & Loch Duich)

The first part of this walk is an historical link between the traditional ferries at Kylerhea to Skye, and Totaig to Dornie, indeed strong walkers can start at Letterfearn and follow a track along the coast as far as Ardintoul, and then undertake this delightful circuit. With ever-changing views of the Loch Alsh coastline for company, and the prospect of spotting an otter, seals, whales, porpoise and dolphin, the circuit is one to linger over. The return stretch from Ardintoul is relatively straightforward and its 4 miles (6.5km) covered fairly quickly.

Just above the small ferry at Glenelg there is a car park above the pier. Start from here and walk to the top end of the parking area and onto a good track. Continue, above Kyle Rhea, and soon pass through gates giving into a plantation, shortly after which the track forks. Branch left, heading towards a huge pylon.

Beyond the pylon, continue on a clear path that eases along at the top of sea slopes dropping to the kyle. The going is delightful, a little boggy in places, but not unduly so. Cross two burns in steep-sided gullies. After the second burn crossing, the on-going path forks again. This time branch right, climbing now to walk alongside a fenceline, and before long reaching the point, Garbhan Cosach Ⓐ. Cross the fence here, and follow a clear path down to the shore.

The view across Loch Alsh is especially pleasing, looking across the heathery knolls of the Balmacara Estate to the distant Applecross hills.

Now simply walk along the shoreline of Camas nan Gall towards Ardintoul Ⓑ.

Loch Alsh and Kyle Rhea

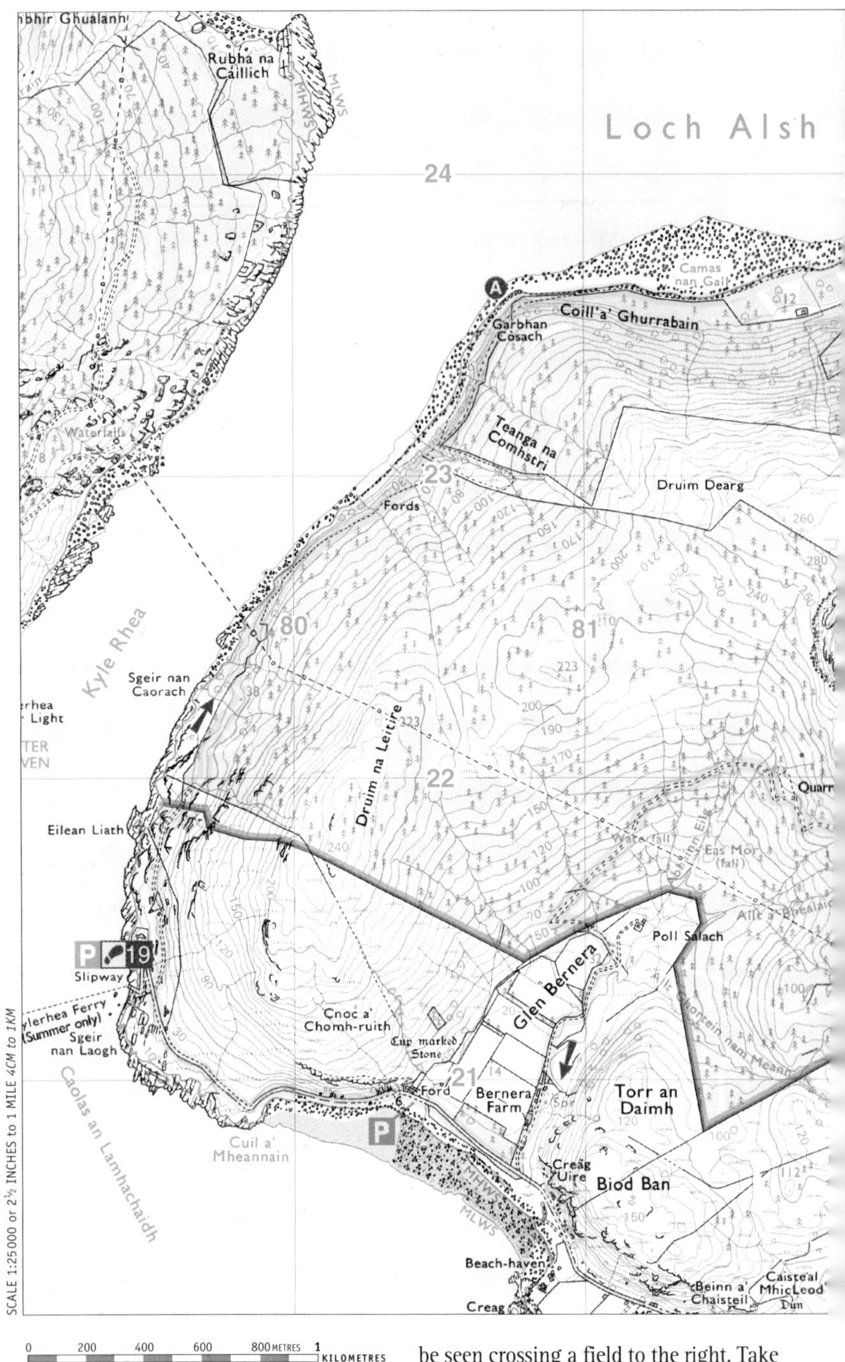

After a forestry gate go alongside a drystone dyke as far as a wall gap (about 440 yds/400m), from where a track can be seen crossing a field to the right. Take to this and on the far side turn left, heading back towards the shore. Pass a large house and turn right onto a clear track that leads upwards, across the north-eastern slopes of Glas Bheinn.

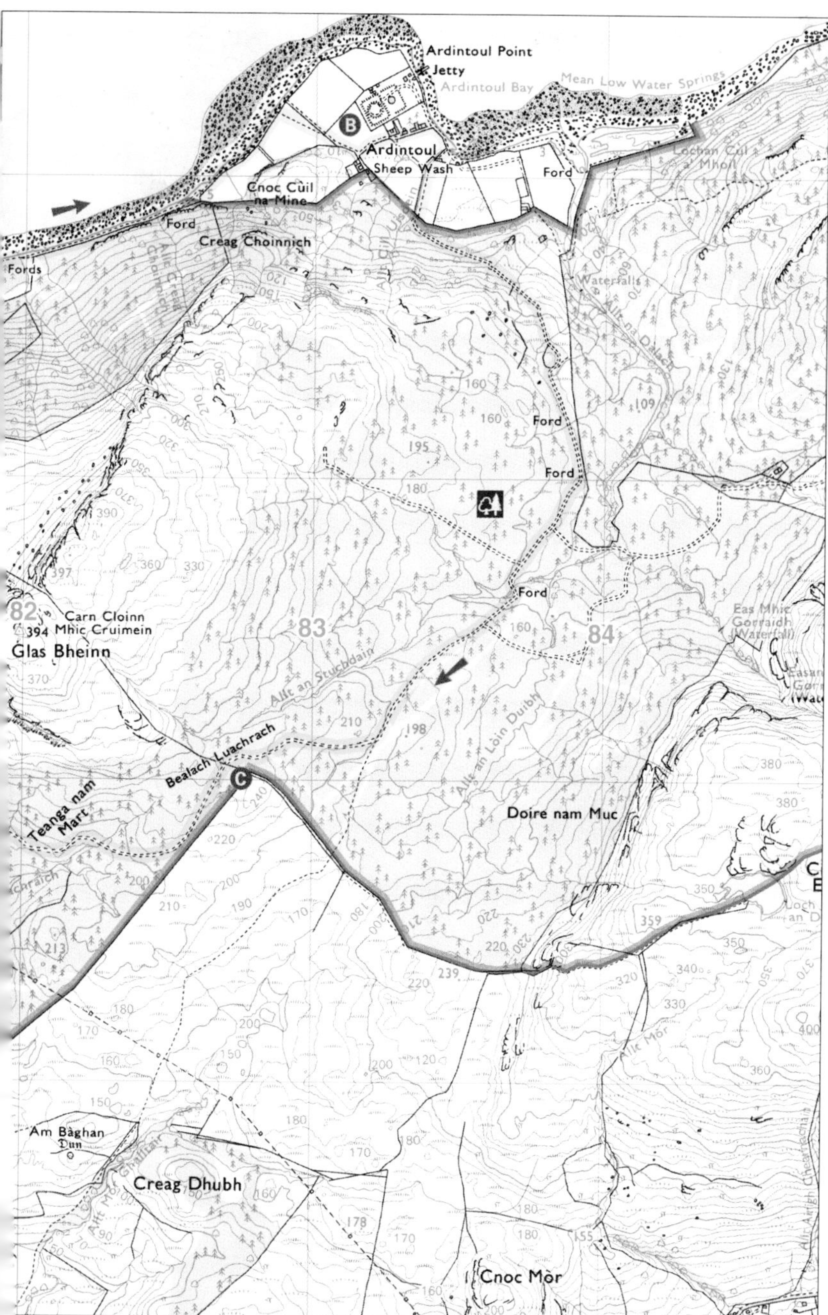

Ardintoul is a small community, but it is said that it was an Ardintoul man who introduced bagpipes to Nepal, with the consequence that the Gurkha regiments still use them to this day.

The steep sections of the track are surfaced, and offer ample opportunity to take a breather and admire the outstanding views. Away to the north-east Eilean Donan Castle stands starkly in front of the white-cottaged village of Dornie and the hills of Kintail, and closer, the whole of Loch Alsh spreads round towards the Kyle of Lochalsh.

The track grinds on steadily to reach its high point at Bealach Luachrach **C** and a fine view of Beinn Sgritheal beyond the bulk of Beinn a'Chapuill. Glenelg Bay and the Sound of Sleat are also visible, a sure sign that the end is almost in sight. From the bealach a fenceline leads unerringly to Glas Bheinn, a 'Marilyn', for those who 'collect' such things, though it is not part of this route. Here, out of sight of Loch Alsh, there is a tremendously invigorating sense of remoteness and tranquillity.

From the bealach it is all downhill, as the track casts about a little before descending into Glen Bernera, pass a farm to reach the valley road. Turn right for about 1 mile (1.6km) of road walking to return to the start. ●

Loch Alsh

Bealach an Sgairne

Start	Morvich
Distance	8 miles (13km) 1900 ft
Approximate time	4 hours
Parking	Kintail Countryside Centre
Refreshments	Shiel Bridge, Dornie
Ordnance Survey maps	Landranger 33 (Loch Alsh, Glen Shiel & Loch Hourn), Explorer 414 (Glen Shiel and Kintail Forest)

The high mountain pass known as the Bealach an Sgairne has been used for centuries, and for a variety of reasons – good, not-so-good and nefarious. The pass is also known as the Gates of Affric and provides a stunning entrance into that region. The ascent is on a good path all the way, and becomes increasingly awesome as the mountains press in on either side towards the end. Here, it may seem strange in an area of outstanding mountains to seek out only a pass between them, but the distance and ascent combined make this an energetic and very satisfying walk, best left for a clear day.

Begin from Morvich, at the Kintail Countryside Centre and walk along the road, going past the caravan site and the turning into Gleann Lichd. When the road surfacing ends, cross a bridge and go forward onto a broad, stony track (signposted 'New Road to the Falls of Glomach'), but leave this quite soon for a path on the right (signposted 'Falls of Glomach').

The path crosses a walled enclosure to a stile beyond which it threads across rough pasture ringed by a deer fence to a gate. Press on across low hillside pastures and then alongside a deer fence above the river. Continue to another deer gate, after which the path heads for Gleann Choinneachain, the Mossy Glen. On reaching another sign for the Falls of Glomach **A**, beside which the path forks, branch right, turning more distinctly into Gleann Choinneachain and heading for another gate.

Beyond the gate the on-going path begins the long ascent to Bealach an

The final section to Bealach an Sgairne

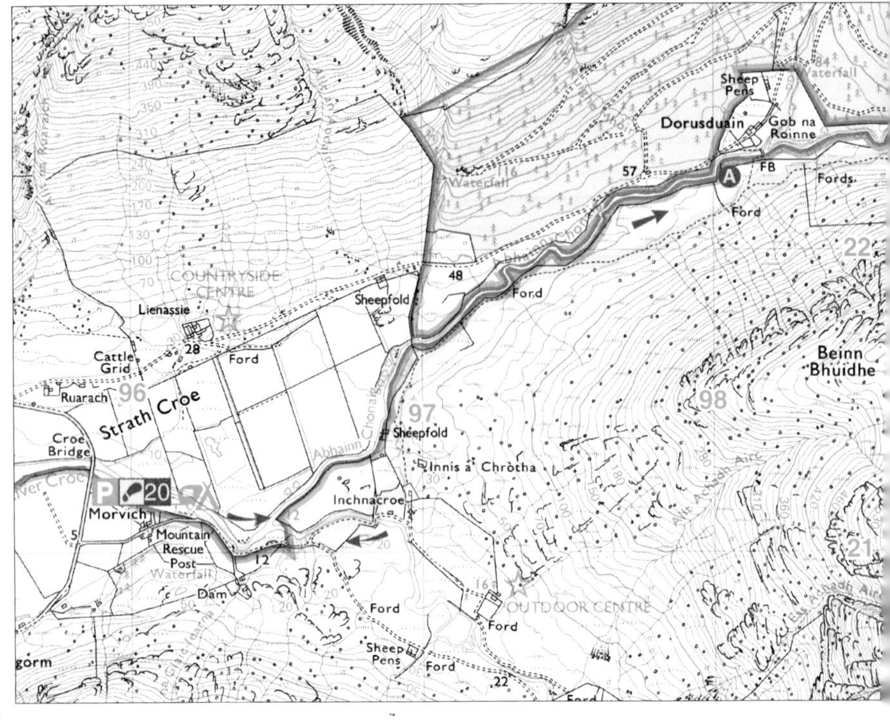

0 200 400 600 800 METRES 1 KILOMETRES
0 200 400 600 YARDS ½ MILES

Sgairne. For a while the path runs parallel with a deer fence high above the Allt Choinneachain, and leads on to a final gate giving into the upper glen.

The glen is remarkably well-endowed with wild flowers: three heathers flourish here, ling, bell heather and cross-leaved heath, along with grass-of-parnassus, tormentil, heath spotted orchid, fragrant orchid, golden saxifrage, selfheal, devil's bit scabious, bog asphodel and common butterwort, the latter an insect-eating plant, the leaves of which engulf its victim, secreting digestive enzymes that break down the hapless insects that chance its way. Butterwort may have got its name from the suggestion that it has been used for curdling milk for butter. It is also supposed to act as a prophylactic against the attentions of fairies and witches.

Looking ahead up the narrowing glen, zigzags appear to the right of the narrow gap leading to the bealach: this is the on-going route. Higher up the glen the path passes through the remains of an old fenceline just below a slabby waterfall composed of burns draining from the slopes and corries of Ben Attow.

The river needs to be forded here **B**, but should not present a problem other than in times of spate. Beyond, a clear path leads up in zigzags, near the top of which a small cairn marks the point of departure of another path. Ignore this, and keep left. From the top of the zigzags, the path goes forward through a narrowing, rocky defile towards the bealach. Finally, the path rises through a tight gorge to the huge cairn that marks the top of the pass, an impressive place.

A little way beyond the top of the pass, a small, cairned top, a convenient place to relax, gives a splendid view of

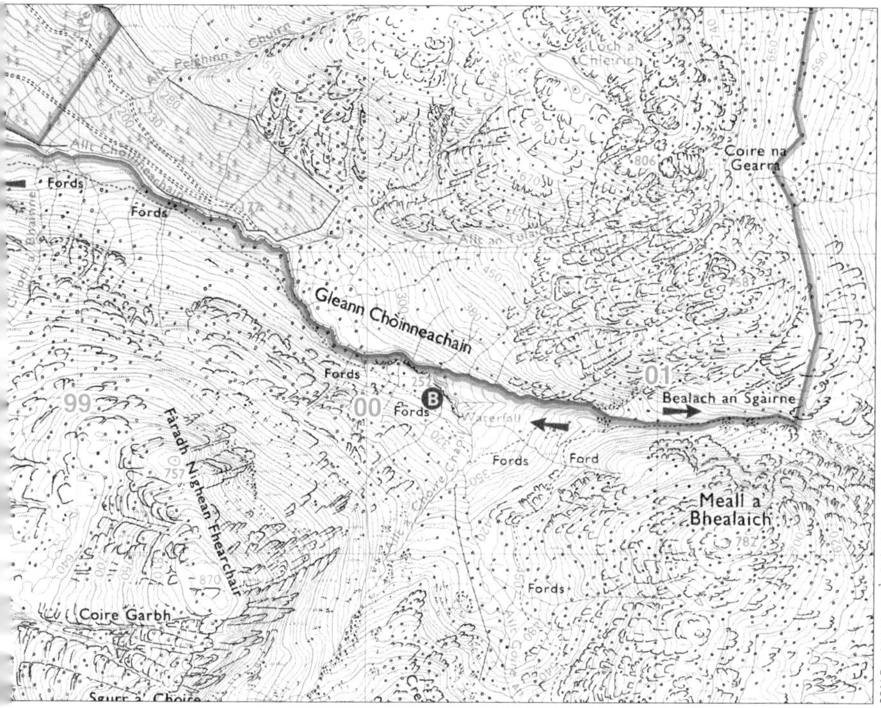

SCALE 1:25 000 or $2\frac{1}{2}$ INCHES to 1 MILE 4CM to 1KM

high mountains and the Loch a'Bhealaich far below. This is a stupendous setting, and certain to thrill anyone who reaches this far.

This pass has seen pedestrian activity for centuries, forming as it does a major east-west route to and from Kintail. All kinds have used it from villains to saints, cattle thieves to drovers, and raiding armies.

The return journey now simply retraces the outward route, but so fascinating is the terrain that it seems not at all like a return journey, more a continuation of the original line.

Heading to Gleann Choinneachain

Bruach na Frithe

Start	Sligachan (Dunvegan road)
Distance	8 miles (13km)
Approximate time	5–6 hours
Parking	Lay-by on Dunvegan road
Refreshments	Sligachan
Ordnance Survey maps	Landranger 32 (South Skye & Cuillin hills), Explorer 411 (Skye – Cuillin Hills)

Walkers wanting for the first time to get a flavour of the Cuillin, will find Bruach na Frithe ideal for the purpose. The summit, which lies only a short distance from rather more difficult ascents on Am Bhastier and Sgurr nan Gillean, is regarded as 'easy', but only in the context of Britain's most complex and demanding range of mountains. The only approach that does not involve scrambling is that through Fionn Choire, and even this is a demanding and energetic exercise, and potentially confusing in poor visibility. The first recorded ascent was in 1845, by Professor James Forbes and Duncan MacIntyre.

Though less obviously a dramatic corrie than others crammed beneath the black crags of the Cuillin, the hummocky expanse of Coire na Circe spreads about the Allt Dearg Mór, and is a traditional cross-country route between Sligachan and Glen Brittle, reached across the Bealach a'Mhaim.

Leave the roadside lay-by, and turn onto a broad track (signposted: 'Footpath to Glen Brittle') that leads to Allt Dearg House. As the house is approached, leave the track and move right, onto a peaty path that can be messy after rain. This stretch, however, is soon passed, and the on-going path improves with height, becoming a stony path on which good progress is made.

The walk beside the Allt Dearg Mór is enlivened by chattering cascades and bright-eyed pools, and is a delight. In poor weather, this riparian ramble, as far as Bealach a'Mhaim, can make a suitable walk in itself.

About ½ mile (800m) before the Bealach a'Mhaim, at a small cairn, the path forks **A**. Here, leave the main path, and go left shortly to cross the burn (Allt Dearg Mór) at an easy ford. Beyond this, a clear path ascends steadily, parallel with the Allt an Fhionn-choire, and heading for Fionn Choire. On reaching the corrie rim, the burn appears ahead in a deep gully, easily crossed to enter the corrie above **B**.

The onward path is now cairned, but not abundantly so. The mountain pass, Bealach nan Lice, lies at the head of the corrie, to the left, with a stony path rising to it. Head in this direction. If

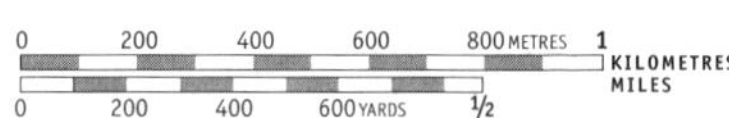

Loch Caol
21
Mountain Rescue Post
Sligachan Hotel
A863
Pipe Line
Weir
Alltdearg House
Ford
Waterfall
Coire Daraich
Allt Coire Daraich
Leathad na Steiseig
Fords
Allt Dearg Mòr
Waterfalls
Coire na Circe
Allt an Uchd Bhuidhe
Allt Dearg Beag
Nead na h-Iolaire
Meall Odhar
Coire Riabhach
Loch a' Choire Riabhaich
Coire a' Bhasteir
Fionn Choire
Sgurr a' Bhasteir
Knight's Peak
Pinnacle Ridge
Sgurr nan Gillean
Am Basteir
Bealach nan Lice
Bealach a' Bhasteir
West Ridge
South East Ridge
Bruach na Frithe
Sgurr a' Fionn Choire
Sgurr na Bhairnich
Sgurr Beag

Sgurr nan Gillean from Bruach na Frithe

going no farther than the corrie there is quite a sizeable arena to explore in which a few small lochans repose. This can be quite a suntrap on a hot day, so be sure to carry plenty of liquid.

To reach the bealach, continue with the path, tending to the left, and rising to meet a bouldery, and then scree, path as the headwall of the corrie is approached. Paths, from Sgurr a'Bhasteir, arrive from the left, joining with the Fionn Choire path just below the bealach **C**. The 'surprise' view of Lota Corrie from the bealach is outstanding. Sgurr a'Fionn Choire stands immediately to the west of the Bealach nan Lice, and is another splendid viewpoint, but its ascent is a scramble of about 150 ft (50m), not a walk.

At the Bealach nan Lice, traverse right, below Sgurr a'Fionn Choire (on the Fionn Choire side), on a good path (take the higher of the two on offer) that leads to a shallow bealach between Sgurr a'Fionn Choire and Bruach na Frithe, where the rest of the main ridge springs into view. The ensuing East Ridge of Bruach na Frithe is no more than a moderate walk, with a little optional scrambling en route. The view from the summit – the only Cuillin summit with a triangulation pillar – is one of the Cuillin's finest.

The only return route, is that by which the ascent was made.

Gleann Lichd

Start	Morvich
Distance	8 miles (12.8km) 500 ft
Approximate time	4 hours
Parking	Morvich Countryside Centre
Refreshments	Shiel Bridge, Dornie
Ordnance Survey maps	Landranger 33 (Loch Alsh, Glen Shiel & Loch Hourn), Explorer 414 (Glen Shiel and Kintail Forest)

On a fine day, the walk into Gleann Lichd, following the course of the River Croe, can seem to go on forever: it is a lovely, wide glen with imposing mountains on either side that host golden eagle and red deer, and has countless places to stop, take pictures, have a picnic or generally ambush good intentions. Nor does the walk suffer from being out-and-back, the glen is a delight to experience in either direction. For the curious, the continuation of the upper glen leads eventually into Glen Affric (see Walk 28).

Begin from the parking area near the Countryside Centre at Morvich and walk along the road, passing a caravan and camping site, as far as a signposted right-of-way on the right for 'Glen Affric via Gleann Lichd' Ⓐ. Here leave the road onto a rough track, through a gate, and heading into the glen.

The early part of the glen has luxurious growths of bog-myrtle (*Myrica gale*), a low, shrubby plant which, long before hops were used to give beer its distinctive bitterness, was used to flavour beer during brewing. The leaves of the bog-myrtle have a pleasant, eucalyptus smell when crushed or broken, and this is said to be a deterrent to insects, especially the Highland 'wee beastie', the midge, which has been known to reduce even the most hardened walkers to tears. Crofters used to wear a sprig of bog-myrtle in their bonnets with uncertain success, and in fairly recent times at least one company on the Isle of Skye started producing an insect repellent cream based on bog-myrtle.

Beside the River Croe

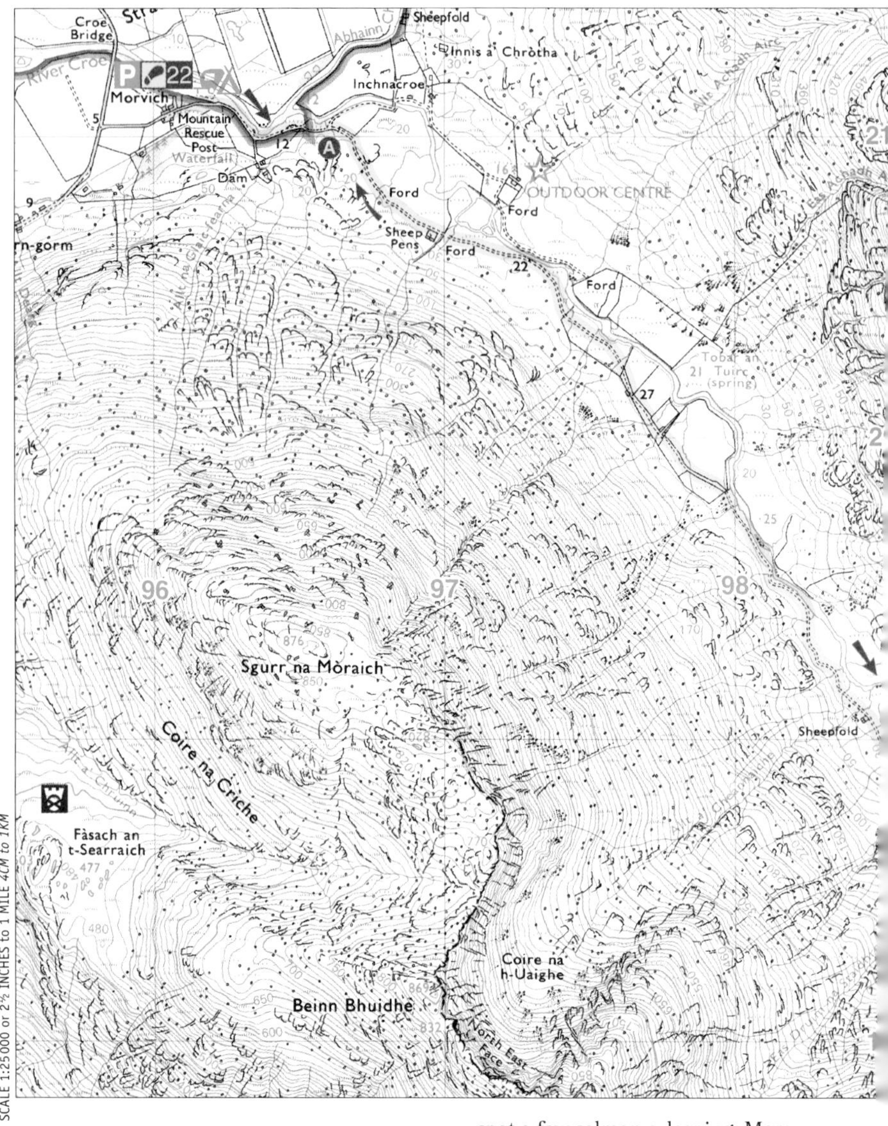

SCALE 1:25 000 or 2½ INCHES to 1 MILE *4CM to 1KM*

0 200 400 600 800 METRES 1 KILOMETRES
MILES
0 200 400 600 YARDS ½

Oil of Lavender has also been recommended as a deterrent, but its strong scent has raised a few eyebrows in passing. In reality, the only true deterrent is wind and rain.

Throughout the walk, the track accompanies the River Croe at varying distances: this is a salmon river and in the early stages of the walk, near a wooded gorge, it may be possible to spot a few salmon a-leaping. More evident are the numerous drystone walls, some built with massive blocks, which betray human endeavour. They are a legacy of the time of the potato famine in the 19th century, and were built by people from Dornie, who walked to the glen each day in return for a bowl of meal.

In times gone by, Glen Lichd was well-populated, though one community on the north side of the river was wiped out by landslide: the site can still be

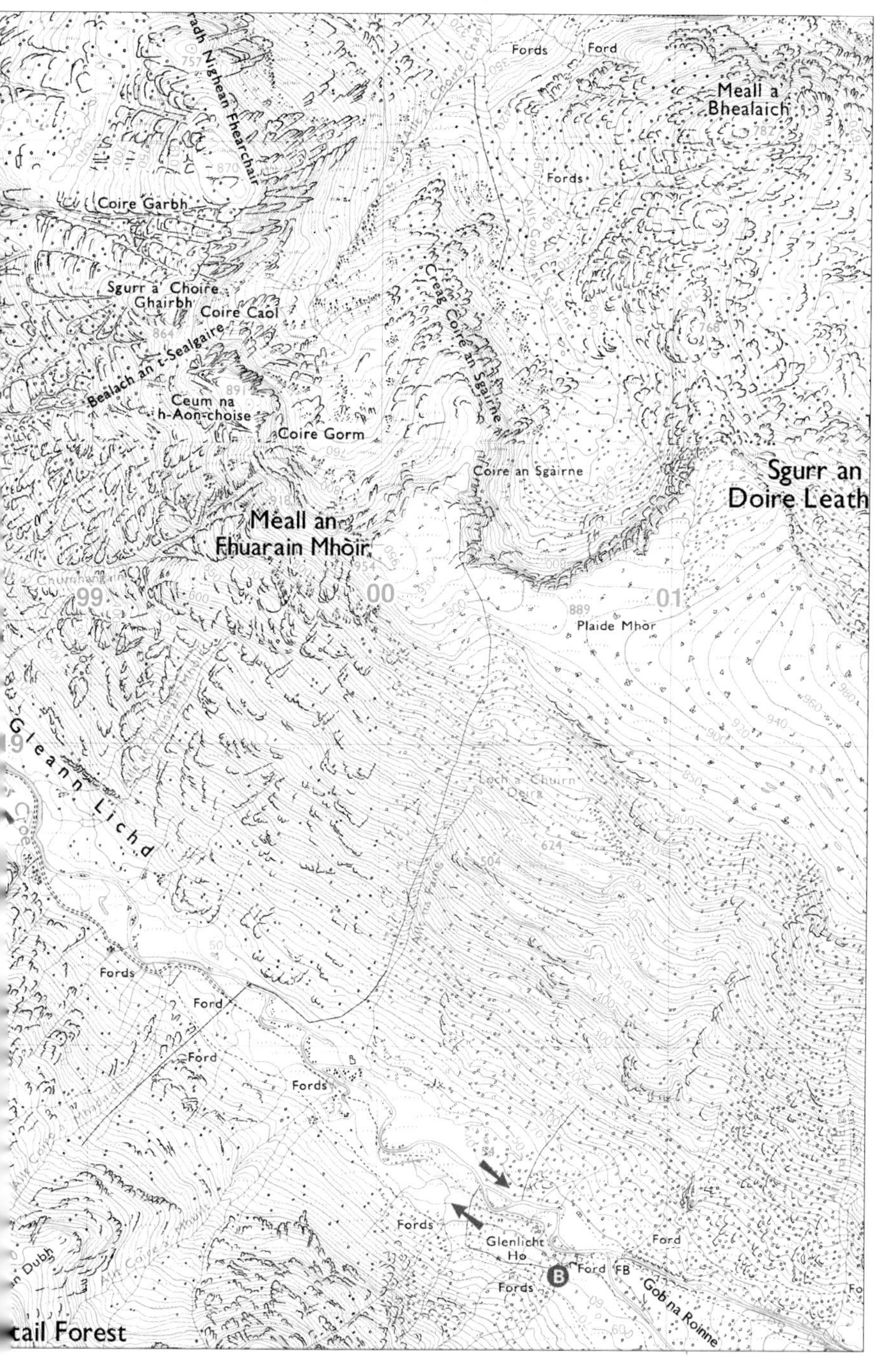

identified, below the slopes of Beinn Fhada.

On the right, heading into the glen, rise the crenallated summits of the Five Sisters of Kintail, which send down steep-sided, alder-hung ravines from their high, slabby ridges.

With simple directness, the track heads all the way up the glen. A final gentle pull brings into view Glenlich

Rowan beside the Croe

House Ⓑ, formerly a keeper's cottage, tucked securely among the hills near the confluence of the Allt Grannda and the Allt an Lapain. The cottage is now known as the Hadden-Woodburn Memorial Hut, opened in May 1956 in memory of Fred Hadden and Elliot Woodburn, who lost their lives in a storm while climbing on Ben Nevis in May 1955. The hut is used by Edinburgh University Mountaineering Club.

Beyond Glen Lichd House, a path leads into the Allt Grannda (and ultimately to Glen Affric), but about 1 mile (1.6km) from the hut it passes above an impressive waterfall. This little add-on is much more rugged than the walk into the glen, and should only be undertaken by experienced rough-terrain walkers.

For everyone, the return journey retraces the outward route, but the whole journey suffers not at all for a second helping of what is a stunning and beautiful glen.

Marsco

Start	Sligachan
Distance	8 miles (13km)
Approximate time	5 hours
Parking	Sligachan
Refreshments	Sligachan
Ordnance Survey maps	Landranger 32 (South Skye & Cuillin Hills), Explorer 411 (Skye – Cuillin Hills)

The distinctive profile of Marsco when viewed from Sligachan is one of the finest sights among the high mountains of Skye; its very independence from other summits gives its bold, sweeping, pyramidal lines great appeal. There are no special difficulties on this ascent, but it is not for novices: expect tough and energetic walking from start to finish. Unlike neighbouring summits, very little scree is encountered on Marsco.

Start from the old bridge at Sligachan, just beyond which a signposted path for Loch Coruisk leads through a gate. The path moves on across a long moorland stretch dominated by the dark gaze of Sgurr nan Gillean. The glen route encounters numerous feeder burns before reaching the rather more substantial Allt na Measarroch. This is the point of departure for Marsco.

Just before the burn, near an old fenceline, there is a path junction **A**. Branch left here, heading up alongside the burn, climbing steadily into the Coire Dubh Measarroch. The path is not always clear, but if lost it is easy enough to follow the course of the burn, climbing all the time to reach the boggy pass, Màm a'Phobuill **B**.

Although shown on maps as Màm a'Phobuill, the Pass of the People, there is a local tradition that this broad bealach is known as The Prince's Pass, Màm a'Phrionnsa, adding weight to the contested theory that the route taken by Bonnie Prince Charlie lay through the glen between Marsco and Beinn Dearg Mheadhonach and into Coire nam Bruadaran, the Corrie of Dreams.

Above the pass, a lovely corrie scoops into the flesh of Marsco. This is Coire nan Laogh, the Corrie of the Calves, and the key to the continuation of the route, and for that matter the start of the return, as the route follows one arm of

Brooding Marsco

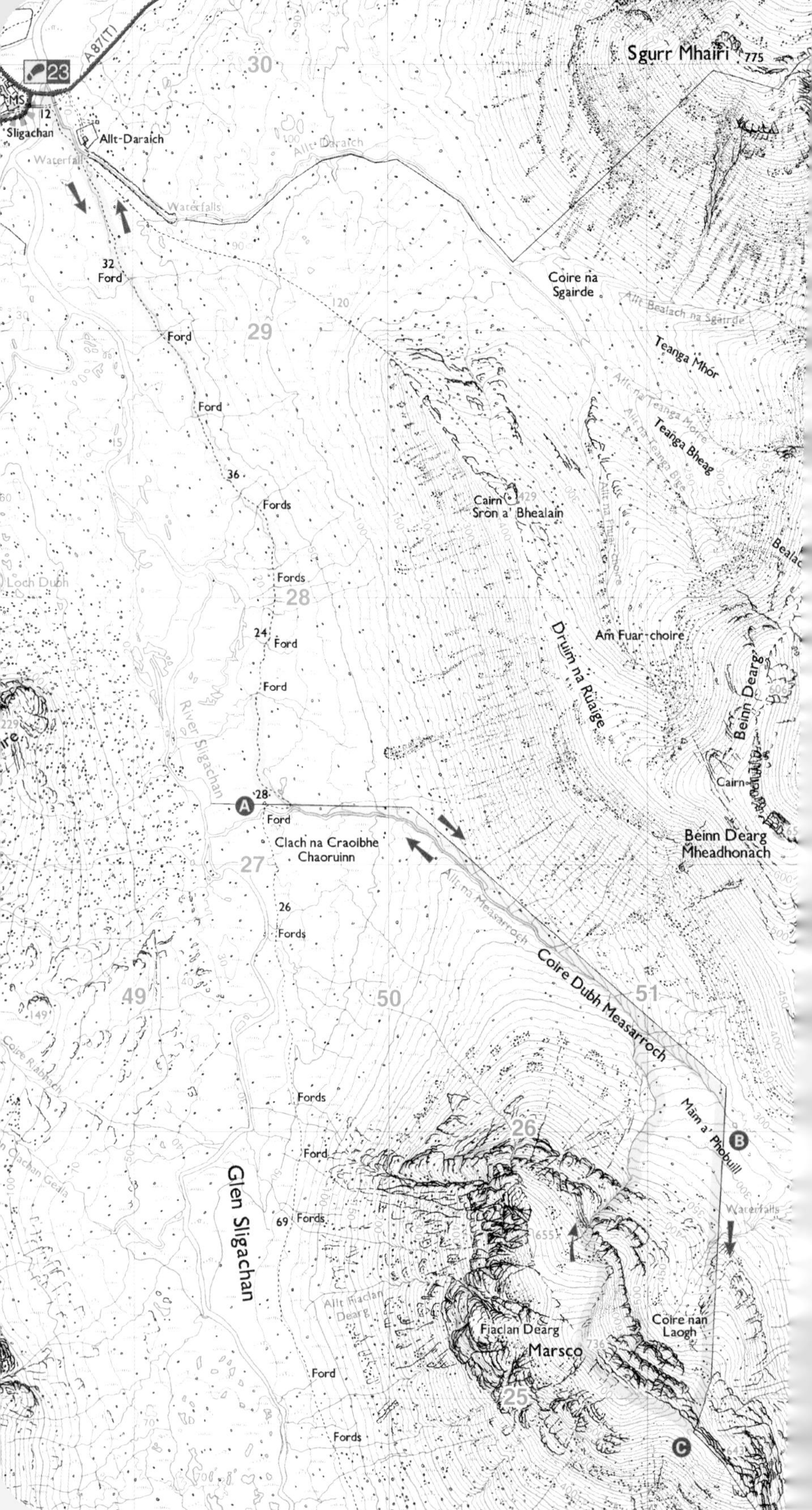

Sgurr Mhairi
775
23
A87(T)
MS
12
Sligachan
Allt-Daraich
Waterfall
Allt Daraich
Waterfalls
30
32
Ford
Coire na
Sgairde
Allt Bealach na Sgairde
29
Ford
Teanga Mhór
Ford
Teanga Bheag
36
Fords
Cairn
429
Sròn a' Bhealain
Loch Dubh
Fords
28
24
Ford
Am Fuar-choire
Druim na Ruaige
Beinn Dearg
Ford
River Sligachan
Cairn
A
28
Ford
Clach na Craoibhe
Chaoruinn
Beinn Dearg
Mheadhonach
27
Allt na Measarroch
26
Fords
Coire Dubh Measarroch
49
50
51
Coire Riabhach
Fords
Màm a' Phobuill
B
26
Ford
Glen Sligachan
Waterfalls
69
Fords
655
Allt Fiaclan
Dearg
Coire nan
Laogh
Fiaclan Dearg
Marsco
736
Ford
25
Fords
C
643

Marsco seen from the top of Bla Bheinn

the corrie going up and the other coming down. If the prospect is too daunting when viewed from Màm a'Phobuill, then simply retreat.

To gain the upward, easterly edge of Coire nan Laogh, cross the Allt Màm a'Phobuill, which issues from the corrie and ends in a waterfall in a deep ravine. Once across the burn, follow a line of old fence posts up the side of the corrie. The ascent is steep and tiring, but not difficult and leads to the south-east ridge of Marsco at a slight dip Ⓒ. From here the way to the summit lies up a narrow ridge; the top is crowned by a modest cairn. Not surprisingly this is a fabulous viewpoint with the Black Cuillin so close, but the bulk of Bla Bheinn and Garbh-bheinn are just as impressive.

From the top of the mountain, start off northwards, then turn north-east down the more northerly arm of the Coire nan Laogh. This is a steeper and rougher option than the way up, especially half-way down, but finally it pans out into a steep rake of grass that in turn feeds into easier slopes above Màm a'Phobuill. Once this bealach is regained, it is simply a question of retreating by the outward route down the Allt na Measarroch to the main path through Glen Sligachan. Having rejoined the glen route, turn right to return to Sligachan.

0 200 400 600 800 METRES 1 KILOMETRES
0 200 400 600 YARDS ½ MILES

Kylerhea Glen circuit

Start	Hardwick
Distance	8¾ miles (14km)
Approximate time	5–6 hours
Parking	Near Kylerhea Otter Centre
Refreshments	Broadford, Glenelg
Ordnance Survey maps	Landranger 33 (Loch Alsh, Glen Shiel & Loch Hourn), Explorer 413 (Knoydart, Loch Hourn & Loch Duich)

This is probably the most demanding walk in this book, a tough and unrelenting circuit of the wild, rugged and beautiful Kylerhea Glen. It should be contemplated only by very strong walkers, and undertaken only in good conditions. But it is a truly satisfying circuit, with stunning views unlikely to have been experienced by many.

With a total of 4250 ft (1295m) of ascent, this walk begins in the vicinity of the Kylerhea Otter Cente, with a direct, very steep and unavoidable assault on the heather, tussock grass and bog-myrtled slopes of Beinn Bhuidhe Ⓐ.

Kyle Rhea, the stretch of water separating Skye from the mainland at Glenelg, is named after Mac an Raeidhinn, one of the legendary Fiennes, or Fianna, who lived near Glenelg and hunted the hills on both sides of the kyle. Legend has it that Fionn and his men were away hunting one day, a task that was proving more and more difficult as their successes over the years had greatly depleted stocks. Yet somehow the women of the clan remained fit and healthy. So Fionn decided to leave one of his men to spy on the women, to see if he could discover the secret of their well-being. Surprisingly, the women were seen to be eating hazel tops, which provided them with considerable nourishment. The smell of food drew Fionn's spy back to the village, where the women fed him. But as soon as he was asleep, they tied him by his hair to a hundred pigs, and shouted to wake him. The warrior, once free of the pigs chased the women into a croft and set fire to it. From

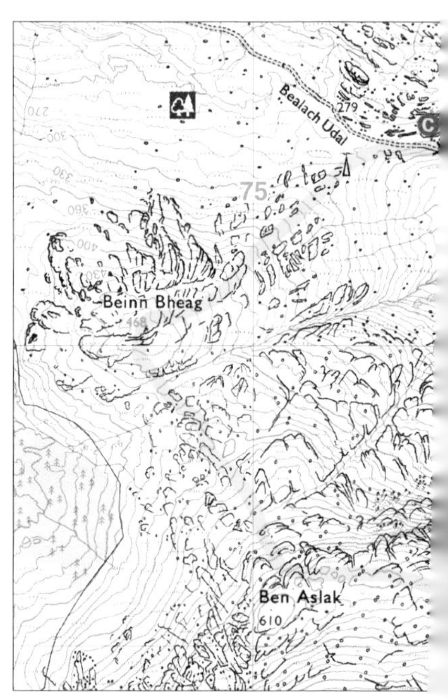

across the kyle, Fionn and his men saw the smoke and raced back to the village, all successfully leaping the sound, except Mac an Raeidhinn, who misjudged his take-off and landed in the water. Ever since, the kyle has borne his name.

The kyle is a valuable sanctuary for wildlife, especially otters, seals and the wide variety of seabirds that visit these coastal waters. Basking sharks, harbour

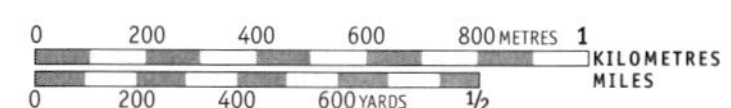

SCALE 1:26316 or about 2½ INCHES to 1 MILE *3.8CM to 1KM*

porpoise and dolphins also pass this way from time to time.

From Beinn Bhuidhe, track below Sgurr na Coinnich to the Bealach nam Mulachag **B**, and from there ascend Beinn na Caillich, the hill of the old woman. Return to the bealach and climb Sgurr na Coinnich, a comparatively easy undertaking given what has gone before.

From Sgurr na Coinnich, descend south-westwards across trackless ground to Bealach Udal **C** on the Broadford-Kylerhea road. Now, cross the road and tackle the heathery slopes of Beinn Bheag, before pressing on to Ben Aslak, a much easier option (see Walk 10). *Walkers jaded after the first two summits should consider simply walking down the road to Kylerhea.* Ben Aslak is not especially demanding, but as the third summit of the walk, its modest pretensions may daunt the weary.

Once the summit of Ben Aslak is gained, head for its eastern top, and from there descend the long and easily-inclined north-east ridge to intersect a coastal path linking Kylerhea with Kinloch Lodge Hotel above Loch na Dal. Head north along this path to reach a bridge over Kylerhea River. Go ahead alongside a fence to reach an unsurfaced road near a house, and there turn right to follow the road out to the main glen road.

Kylerhea Glen from Bealach Udal

Suisnish and Boreraig

Start	Kilchrist (Cill Chriosd) church, Strath Suardal.
Distance	10 miles (16km) or 7 miles (11km)
Approximate time	5 hours
Parking	Kilchrist
Refreshments	Broadford
Ordnance Survey maps	Landranger 32 (South Skye & Cuillin Hills), Explorer 412 (Skye – Sleat)

Few places on Skye bear such evident testimony to the ruthlessness that underpinned the Highland Clearances as the deserted villages of Suisnish and Boreraig. This walk, which begins from the ruined church of Strath, at Kilchrist, visits both communities. It is a sad and poignant excursion, made bearable only by outstanding coastal scenery and the chance of spotting a golden eagle above the cliffs of Carn Dearg. The walk can be shortened, avoiding all the road walking, by driving to Camas Malag and beginning from there. This gives an out-and-back walk to Boreraig, a maximum of 7 miles (11km).

Part way down Strath Suardal stands the ruined church of Cill Chriosd, ivy- and cotoneaster-clad, surrounded by a graveyard much older than the church, and which may date from prehistoric times. The church, the former parish church of Strath, evidently existed in the early 16th century, and probably during the late 15th, but had ceased to be used by 1840, because of its state of disrepair.

From the church, set off along the narrow road, heading for Torrin and Kilbride, for about 1½ miles (2.5km) *taking care against approaching traffic.* The road walking is unavoidable, if doing the complete circuit, but it provides excellent views of Bla Bheinn and Clach Glas, initially across the reed-filled waters of Loch Cil Chriosd.

Loch Cill Chriosd is said to be haunted by a terrible monster which laid waste to the land, and carried off and devoured women and children. Not until St Maelrhuba blessed the waters of the loch was the monster laid to rest, since when the loch waters are said to have held great healing powers.

Finally, as the road bends right, leave it for a lane on the left (A) that leads to the rocky shores of Loch Slapin and the tiny cove of Camas Malag, where the road surfacing ends.

A fine walk ensues, along a clear and broad track, built when the Board of Agriculture re-crofted Suisnish during the early part of the 20th century. Briefly, the track turns inland a little to negotiate the goat-willowed burn of Glen Boreraig, before resuming its southerly course for Suisnish.

Once more the track turns inland as it crosses the Allt Poll a'Bhainne (B), near which the hut circle marked on the map is revealed as a pile of rocks on a slight rise. Shortly after crossing the Allt Poll a'Bhainne, the track approaches Suisnish, with many of the crofting enclosures and field-boundary dykes still in evidence, and a wide spread of rich, tormentil-dotted grassland, scarcely reclaimed by weeds, that defines the extent of this small community. One ruined croft, beside its protective shield of rowan trees, is rather more substantial than the others, but a forlorn sight nonetheless, and home now only to sheep and summer swallows. Beyond this, the track runs on to a sheep washing station, where it ends.

Past this station, a path, not easy to locate, heads for the top of a small sea cliff, before passing south of Carn Dearg, and descending to the shore and a natural rock pavement.

The on-going route is then clear, and leads all the way to Boreraig, passing two fine waterfalls en route, and trekking below the southernmost, eagle-patrolled escarpments of Beinn Bhuidhe.

As you enter the ruins of Boreraig **C**, head for the conspicuous standing stone, almost central to the triangle of arable land that presses northwards into the flanks of Beinn a' Mheadhain.

The clearance of Suisnish and Boreraig was one of the most brutal episodes in an already tragic history of the Highland Clearances. The chief culprit was the factor to Lord MacDonald, Ballingall, who in 1852 found his way to these old Skye communities where Loch Slapin and Loch Eishort meet. If the crofters offered resistance, they were forcibly evicted and their properties razed to the ground to prevent them from returning. One

0 200 400 600 800 METRES 1 KILOMETRES
MILES
0 200 400 600 YARDS ½

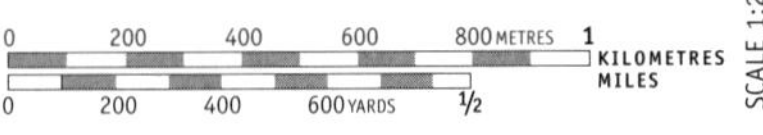

SCALE 1:25 000 or 2½ INCHES to 1 MILE 4CM to 1KM

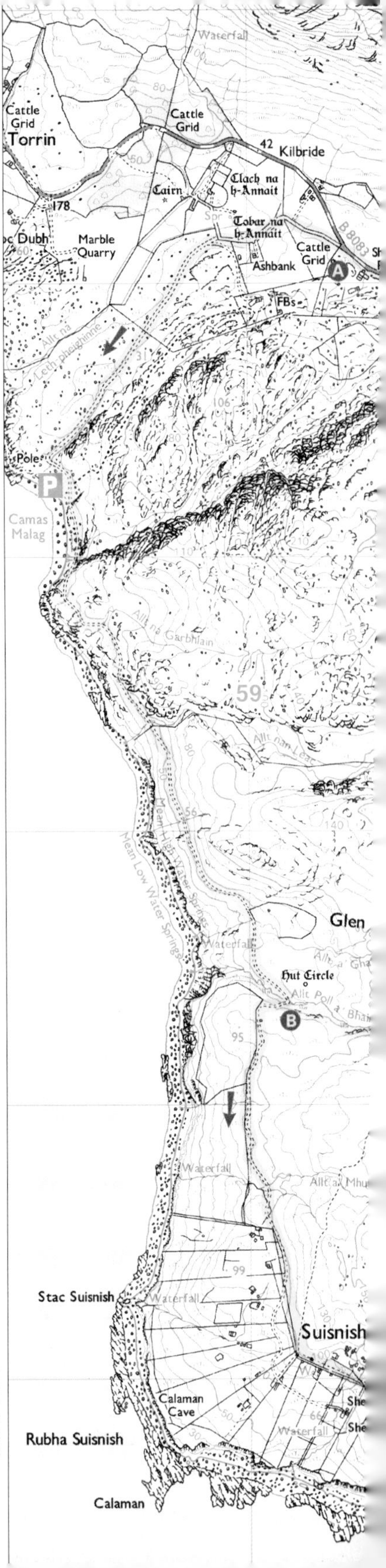

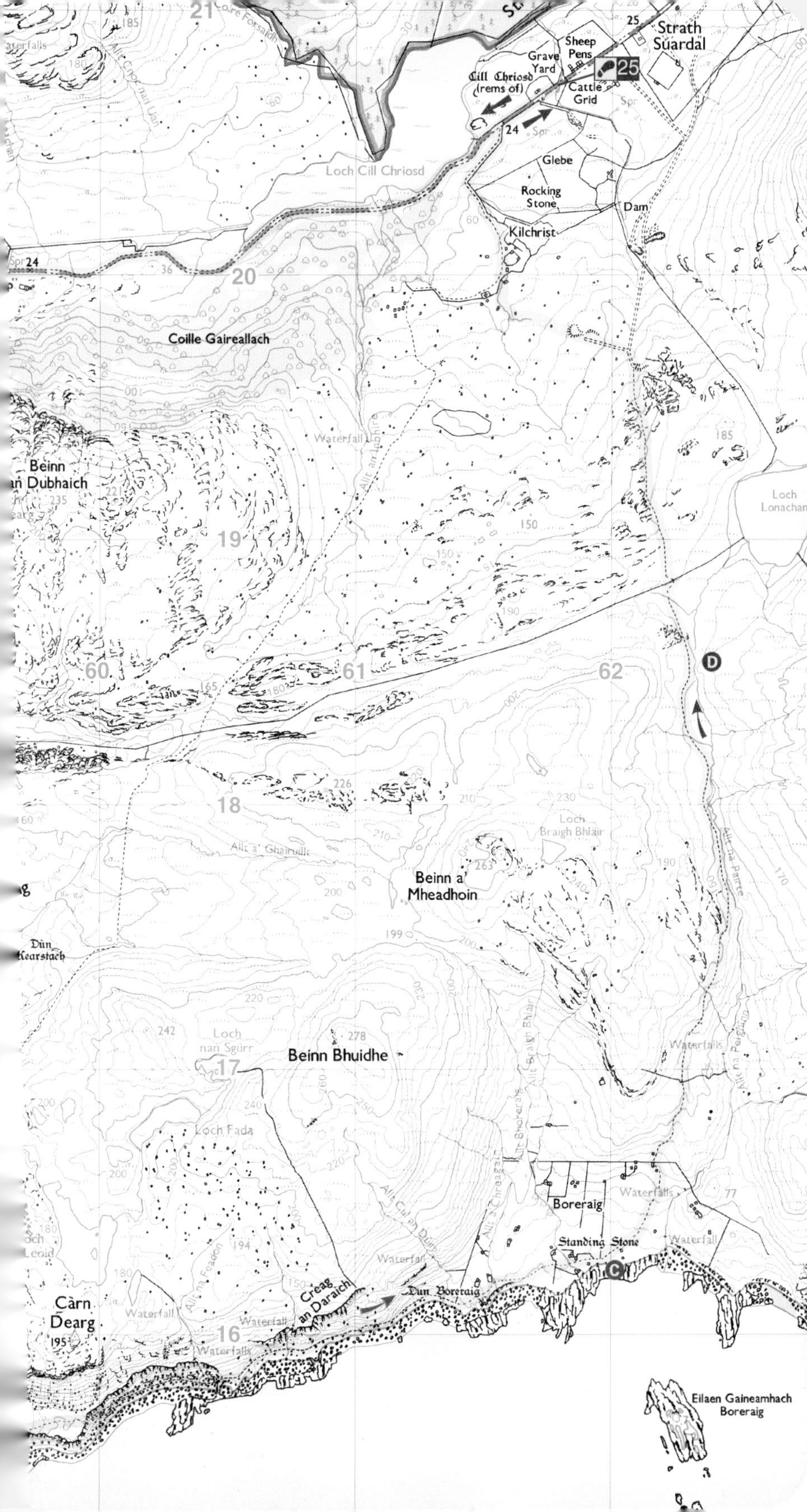

Strath Suardal
Sheep Pens
Grave Yard
Cill Chriosd (rems of)
Cattle Grid
25
24
Glebe
Rocking Stone
Dam
Loch Cill Chriosd
Kilchrist
Coille Gaireallach
Beinn an Dubhaich
Waterfall
Allt an Inbhire
Loch Lonachan
D
60
61
62
19
20
21
18
Allt a' Ghairuillt
Loch Braigh Bhlair
Beinn a' Mheadhoin
Allt na Pairte
Dùn Kearstach
Loch nan Sgùrr
Beinn Bhuidhe
Loch Fada
Allt Bhorerai
Allt Braigh Bhlair
Allt a' Chreagain
Allt Cul an Dùin
Waterfalls
Boreraig
Standing Stone
C
Dùn Boreraig
Creag an Daraich
Allt na Feadon
Càrn Dearg
Waterfall
16
17
Eilaen Gaineamhach Boreraig

Kilchrist church

was an old man of 86. He said: 'I have paid 66 rents to the MacDonalds, and I am not one farthing in arrears. To be cast out of my house and my home to make room for...sheep is what I never expected. It is breaking my heart.'

Having explored the village, either retrace the outward route (if starting at Camas Malag) or return to the standing stone, and from it follow a fairly obvious path, north-east and north, passing more ruined houses, eventually to join a good, if wet, path above the Allt na Pairte. In the middle of the moorland a stile spans a fence. This marks the boundary of the Beinn Nan Carn Native Woodland, planted in 2000 with the intention of replicating the native woodland. All the trees planted, almost a quarter of a million, were grown from Skye seeds of the trees typical of the climate and region – ash, oak, willow, holly, hazel, aspen, alder, rowan and birch. The fence is there to protect the young trees from deer and sheep.

This path now strikes across the moors, is rarely dry, and wettest in the vicinity of Loch Lonachan. But once past this, the going improves as it climbs to a watershed Ⓓ and then descends into Strath Suardal against the rugged backdrop of Bla Bheinn and Clach Glas.

A number of paths lead down to the Strath road, the most interesting taking you by way of a marble quarry that supplied some of the stone for the abbey on Iona, before emerging through willow scrub on to the road, not far from the start.

man, who did return to Suisnish, was found dead at the door of his ruined house the next morning, having perished from the cold during the night. Ballingall argued that the laird had been 'over-indulgent' allowing the community to waste good land, and that 'it would be better for them and it if they were removed.' Incredibly, one of the evicting officers announced that in directing the evictions, Lord MacDonald was 'prompted by motives of benevolence, piety and humanity, because they were too far from the church.' Most of the people were sent to Campbeltown, where they were put aboard the Hercules by the Emigration Commissioners. Many died from smallpox, and on hearing this the 32 families still at Suisnish and Boreraig asked that they should be left to stay on Skye. They were threatened with eviction in the autumn of 1853.

Eighteen people were somehow still surviving at Boreraig and Suisnish when the spring of 1854 arrived, but by the first days of summer, the township was deserted. One of the last to leave

Srath Mór and Srath Beag

Start	Head of Loch Slapin, near Abhainn an t-Sratha Mhóir
Distance	10½ miles (17km)
Approximate time	5–6 hours
Parking	At start
Refreshments	Torrin, Broadford
Ordnance Survey maps	Landranger 32 (South Skye & Cuillin Hills), Explorer 411 (Skye – Cuillin Hills)

Despite both running north-south, the two glens of Srath Mór and Srath Beag, typical Highland glens, contrive to link the east and west coast of Skye. Between them they enclose a minor summit, Beinn na Cro, an optional add-on for the energetic. This is the route (in part) taken by Bonnie Prince Charlie as he journeyed across Skye in 1746, bound for the safety of France. In times of spate it is difficult if not impossible to cross the Abhainn an t-Sratha Mhóir when the path switches sides near the lochan.

From the roadbridge spanning the Abhainn an t-Sratha Mhóir set off along a clear stony track, soon passing Clach Oscar (Oscar's Stone), a large split boulder tossed here by Oscar, son of Ossian, one of the legendary Fiennes, or Fianna, in a moment of merriment. The track soon reaches the shores of Loch na Sguabaidh, where, after rain, it can often be flooded.

Loch na Sguabaidh used to be inhabited by a waterhorse that preyed upon any pretty girl who wandered within his reach. Plain lassies were thought to be safe enough; indeed, to have been captured by the waterhorse and to have escaped was to assure a reputation as a beauty. The waterhorse's taste for mischief, however, eventually led to his demise, as, en route to Loch na Creitheach, the beast was killed by MacKinnon of Strath in Bealach na Beiste (the Pass of the Beast).

Beyond the loch the path remains clear but is in poor condition, though it never climbs higher than 55 ft (17m). At Lochan Stratha Mhóir **A** the path

Clach Oscar

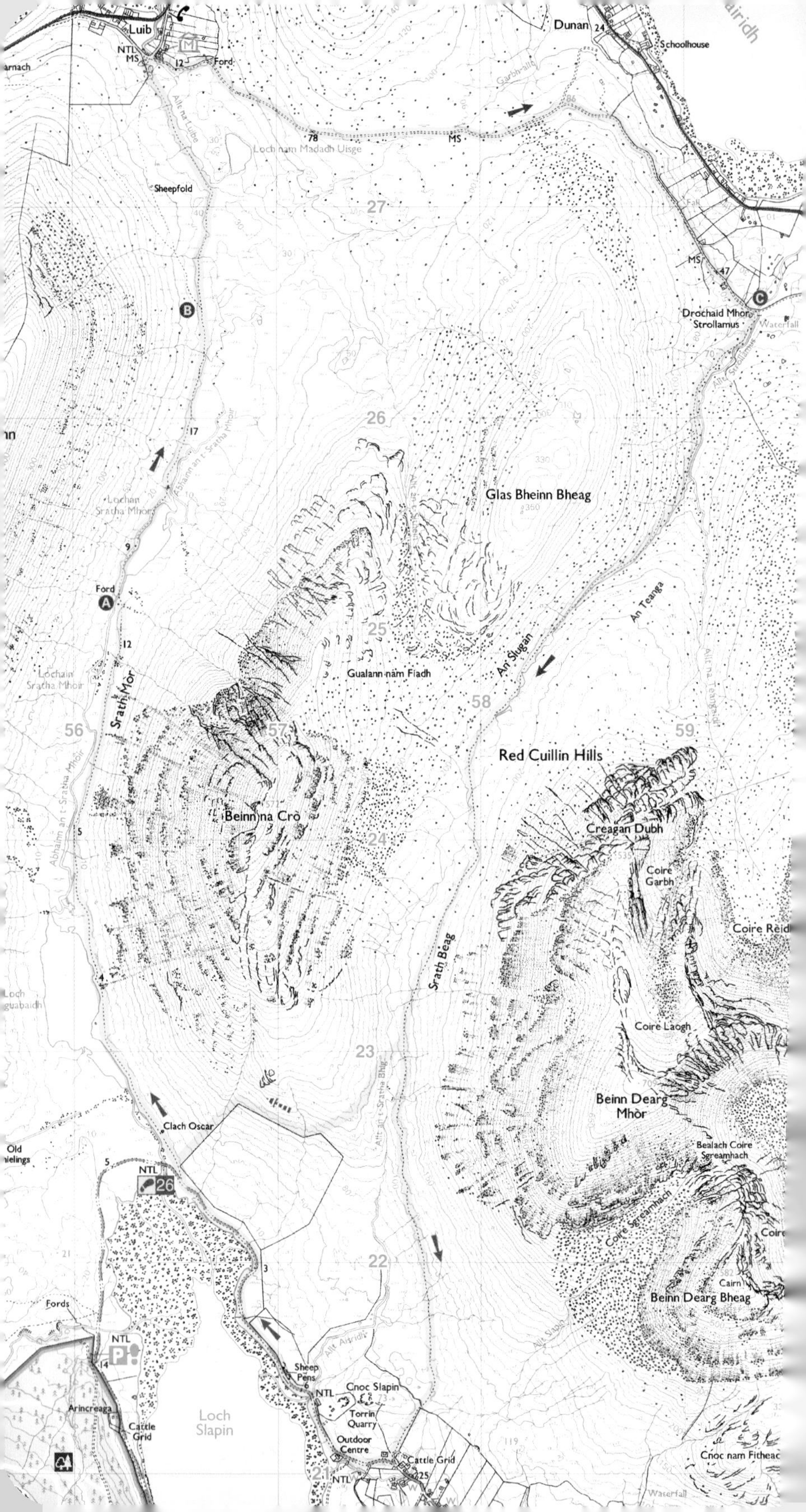

Luib
NTL
MS
Ford
Dunan
Schoolhouse
Loch nam Madadh Uisge
Sheepfold
MS
Drochaid Mhor
Strollamus
Waterfall
Glas Bheinn Bheag
Lochan Sratha Mhoir
Ford
Lochain Sratha Mhoir
Srath Mòr
Gualann nam Fiadh
An Slugan
An Teanga
Red Cuillin Hills
Beinn na Cro
Creagan Dubh
Coire Garbh
Coire Reidh
Srath Beag
Coire Laogh
Beinn Dearg Mhòr
Bealach Coire Sgreamhach
Coire Sgreamhach
Beinn Dearg Bheag
Cairn
Clach Oscar
Old Shielings
Fords
Arincreaga
Cattle Grid
Loch Slapin
Sheep Pens
Cnoc Slapin
Torrin Quarry
Outdoor Centre
Cattle Grid
Cnoc nam Fitheach
Waterfall

Heading into Strath Mór

switches sides of the glen, though the crossing point is not distinct, and may be impossible to follow if the river is swollen. (*In such a state, retreat is the only sensible option, as deviating from such path as there is can be dangerous given the preponderance of sink holes through the glen.*)

Once safely across, the path drops gently as it heads for Luib, a former crofting hamlet, now with a small crofting museum. Approaching Luib, the path forks Ⓑ. Branch right, taking the most direct route to the village.

On reaching the road, go immediately right, but as the road bends left, leave it at a gate for the old Broadford-Portree road, which now climbs across the southern slopes of Am Meall, north of Loch nam Madadh Uisge, and provides much improved going as far as the Allt Strollamus Ⓒ. This old highway is not, however, a right-of-way, and so it is important for visitors to ensure that all gates are left as found.

Leave the old road here, but do not cross the river, keeping instead to its east bank, along a path that climbs into the narrows of An Slugan. Rather more ascent is ahead, rising to about 623 ft (190m) to reach a wide, grassy bealach where the path switches sides as in Srath Mór.

Now press on down Srath Beag, high above the true left bank of Allt an t-Sratha Bhig, to reach the road at Torrin. Turn right and follow the road back to the start.

The finish can be shortened by recrossing the Allt an t-Sratha Bhig towards the southern end of Srath Beag, and climbing across rough ground, following the boundary of a large fenced enclosure directly to the starting point.

0 200 400 600 800 METRES 1 KILOMETRES
0 200 400 600 YARDS ½ MILES

Gleann Beag

Start	Eilanreach
Distance	12 miles (19km) (from Eilanreach) or 5½ miles (9km) (from Balvraid)
Approximate time	3–6 hours
Parking	Eilanreach or Balvraid (both limited)
Refreshments	Glenelg
Ordnance Survey maps	Landranger 33 (Loch Alsh, Glen Shiel & Loch Hourn), Explorer 413 (Knoydart, Loch Hourn & Loch Duich)

Gleann Beag, tucked neatly away south of Glenelg, holds considerable fascination, a place of verdant loveliness and not inconsiderable prehistory. There is, too, a gentle ruggedness about the place, influenced greatly by the accompanying sounds of the glen river and the air of distance from outside influences. This walk can be as long or as short as wished: either walking in from Eilanreach or driving in as far as Balvraid to continue to the minor summit, but splendid viewpoint, of Torr Beag.

Between Eilanreach and Balvraid the road through Gleann Beag is narrow but surfaced, and it leads alongside the river, past the usually impressive waterfall of Eas Mor Chuil an Duin, to Dun Telve **A** and Dun Troddan, both substantial remains of brochs (circular fortifications) built about 2000 years

Glenelg

ago. Both sites are open and may be freely visited.

Very little is known about brochs, which may go some way to explaining why they are such fascinating structures: the skill of the craftsmen who built them is something to be wondered at, and admired. No one knows why they were built, though the assumption is that they were intended to protect, or stand as status symbols. Certainly in Iron Age times there was considerable intertribal conflict, and some means of protecting one's own tribe and its stock would have been necessary. That few brochs seem to have been completely demolished suggests that they were certainly very effective deterrents to Iron Age rampaging. The name 'broch' derives from the Old Norse language, which means a strong or fortified place. But brochs have nothing to do with the Norse/Viking invaders, who first came to Britain around AD 800, for the brochs of Scotland were built between the first century BC and the first century AD. By the time of the Vikings, brochs had long since gone out of use, but the Vikings saw them as forts of some kind, hence the name. About half of the stonework of the Dun Telve broch in Gleann Beag remains intact, though some stones were almost certainly plundered for the building of the Bernera Barracks at Glenelg.

Beyond Dun Telve lies Dun Troddan, perched rather higher on the valley side, and then the road runs on to the farmstead at Balvraid. Here the road

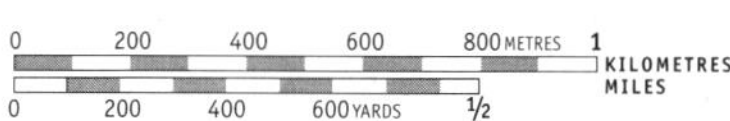

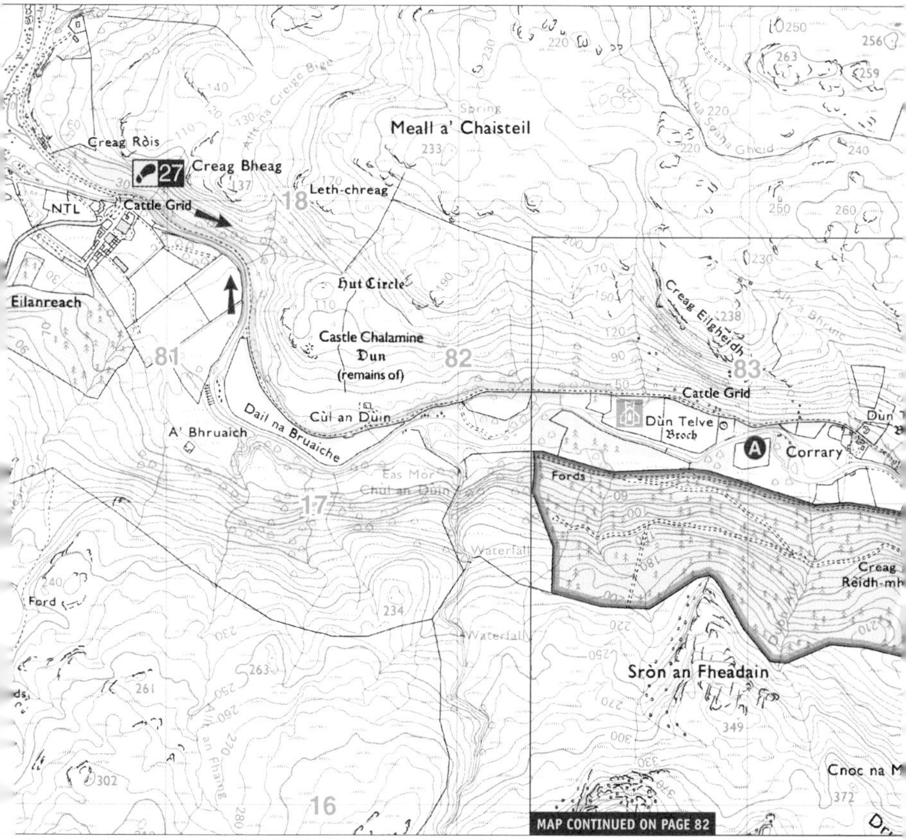

MAP CONTINUED ON PAGE 82

surfacing ends, but a good track continues above the river and climbs gently to pass Dun Grugaig, an unusual D-shaped broch. This style of broch-building is thought to pre-date the conventional, circular brochs.

Onwards the route is a delight to follow and remains full of intrigue. At Srath a'Chomair Ⓑ, a side glen, Aoidhdailean, leads south-east to the head of Arnisdale and Kinloch Hourn, a drove route, surveyed by Thomas Telford, and through which cattle were to be brought en route to lowland trysts, though the route was never used. A little farther on Ruighe na Corpaich, the ridge of the corpses, marks a spot where the coffins of deceased bound for burial in Glenelg would be rested, a kind of Highland lychgate.

The track continues northwards now, crossing a burn Ⓒ issuing from Loch Iain Mhic Aonghais, which is named after John MacInnes, who drowned in the loch. The track climbs to a low pass west of Torr Beag, from which the summit is easily attained. This, too, has prehistoric significance, as tumbledown defences on the north-east slopes testify.

From this summit, a splendid viewpoint, the return is simply by the outward route. Walkers who can arrange transport, might consider continuing across the pass into Glen More to rejoin the Old Military Road serving the Bernera Barracks not far from the modern road leading out of the glen over Mam Ratagan. ●

0 200 400 600 800 METRES 1 KILOMETRES
0 200 400 600 YARDS ½ MILES

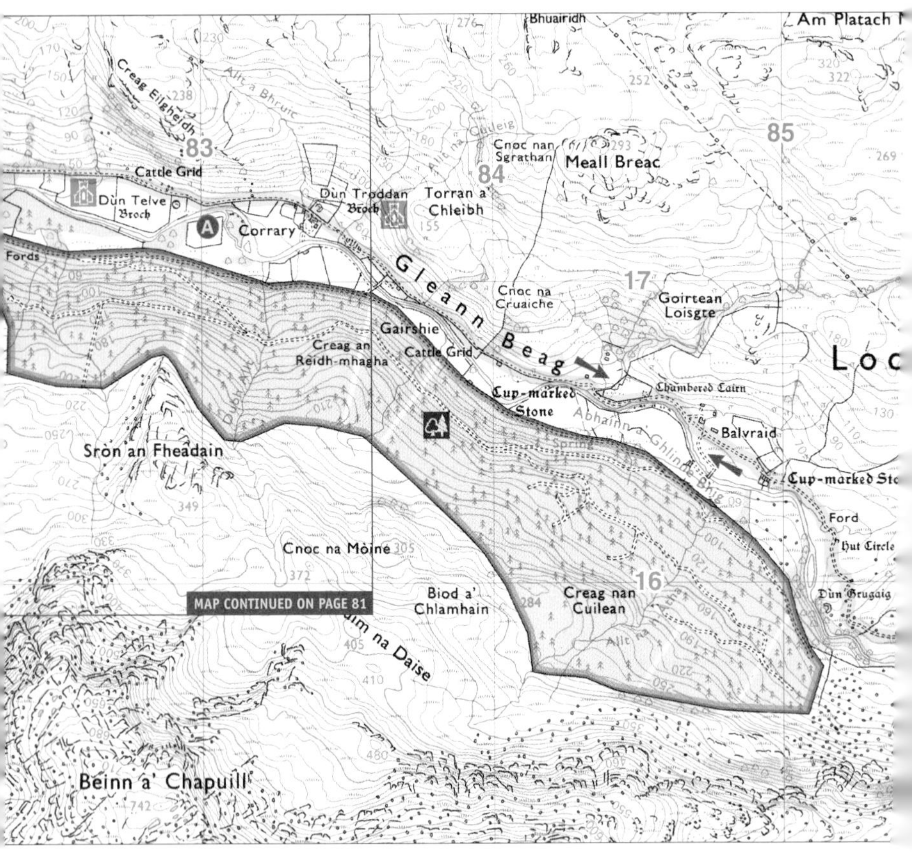

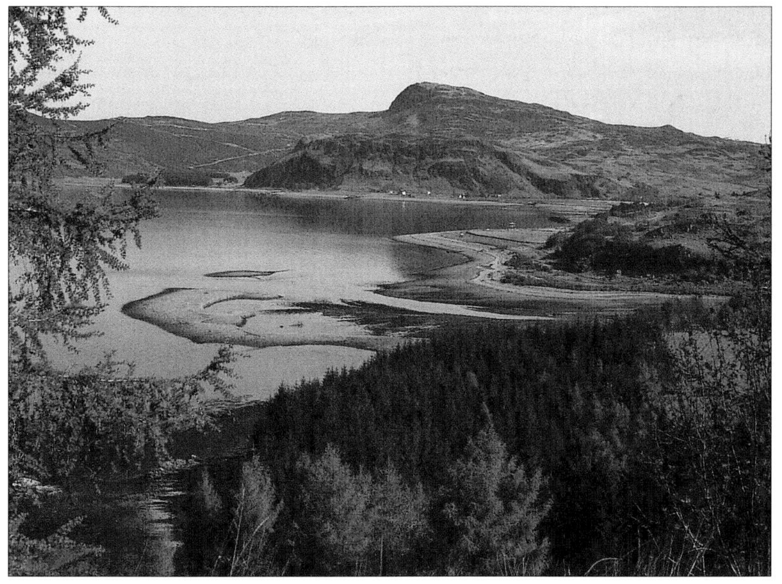

The bay at Glenelg

SCALE 1:25 000 or 2½ INCHES to 1 MILE *4CM to 1KM*

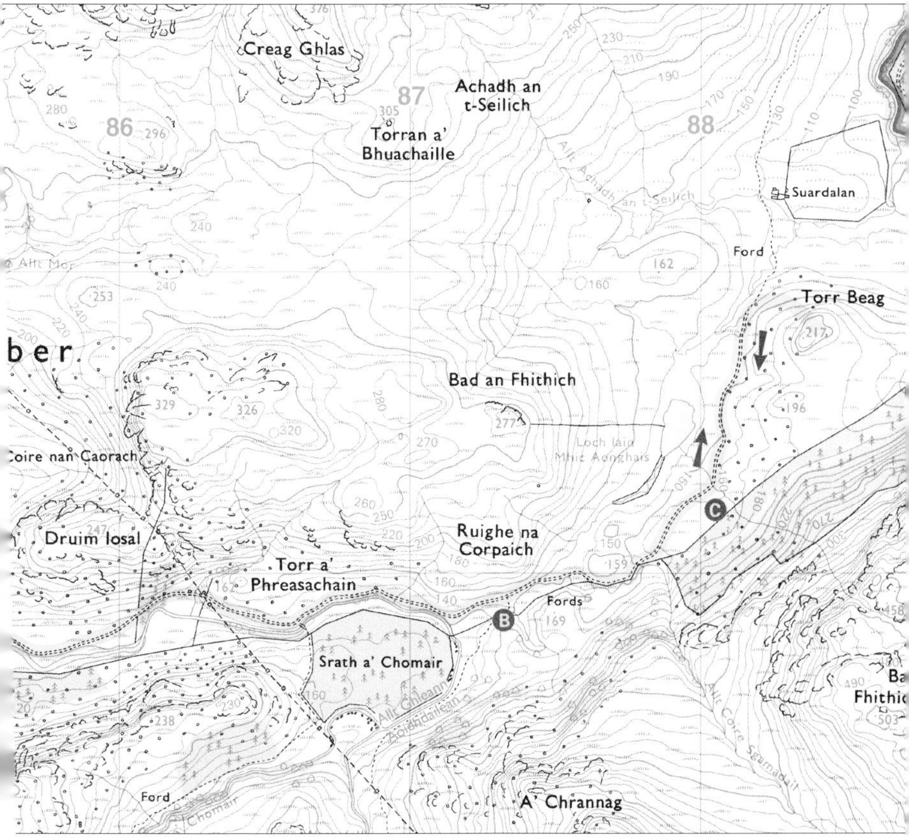

Creag Ghlas
Achadh an t-Seilich
Torran a' Bhuachaille
Allt Achadh an t-Seilich
Suardalan
Ford
Allt Mor
Torr Beag
Bad an Fhithich
Loch Iain Mhic Aonghais
Coire nan Caorach
Druim Iosal
Torr a' Phreasachain
Ruighe na Corpaich
Fords
Srath a' Chomair
Allt Gleann Aoidhdailean
Allt Coire Sgamadail
A' Chrannag
Ford

Into Glen Affric

Start	Loch Cluanie
Distance	15 miles (24km)
Approximate time	8 hours
Parking	Lay-by on A87 1 mile (1.6km) east of Cluanie Inn
Refreshments	Cluanie Inn, Shiel Bridge
Ordnance Survey maps	Landranger 33 (Loch Alsh, Glen Shiel & Loch Hourn), Explorer 414 (Glen Shiel & Kintail Forest)

This long and splendid walk touches only briefly on the western edge of Glen Affric, but provides a scintillating route between the high mountains, across the British watershed and out through Gleann Lichd to end at Morvich. Park a car filled with comfort food and drink at the Kintail Countryside Centre at Morvich as an incentive, and then get a lift to Cluanie – taking a sackful of comfort food and drink for the journey. Expect to be a long time, and to enjoy the experience. There are good paths throughout, but the walk is best left for a clear day.

Just beyond the point where the Allt a'Chaorainn Mhóir reaches Loch Cluanie, go through a gate onto a track rising steadily into the long glen of An Caorann Mór. The route climbs easily enough, crossing countless burns that can make the walk a wet experience. On the left rises the steep-sided Am Bàthach, a double-topped summit; to the right the long ridge linking two very

The track leading over into Gleann Lichd

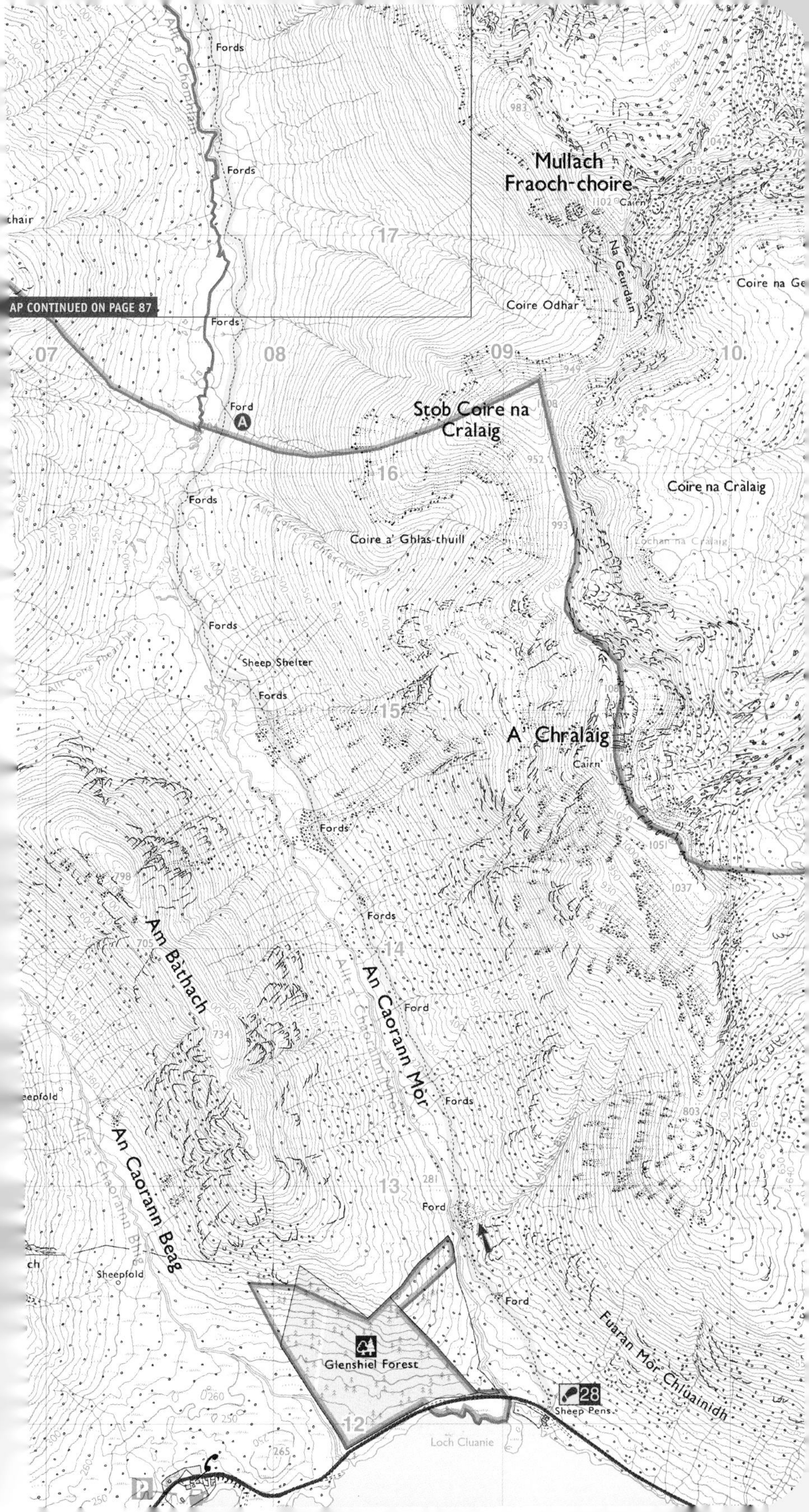

AP CONTINUED ON PAGE 87
Mullach Fraoch-choire
Stob Coire na Cràlaig
A' Chràlaig
Am Bàthach
An Caorann Mòr
An Caorann Beag
Fuaran Mòr Chluainidh
Coire Odhar
Na Geurdain
Coire na Cràlaig
Lochan na Cràlaig
Coire a' Ghlas-thuill
Sheep Shelter
Sheepfold
Sheep Pens
Glenshiel Forest
Loch Cluanie
Fords
Ford
Cairn
28

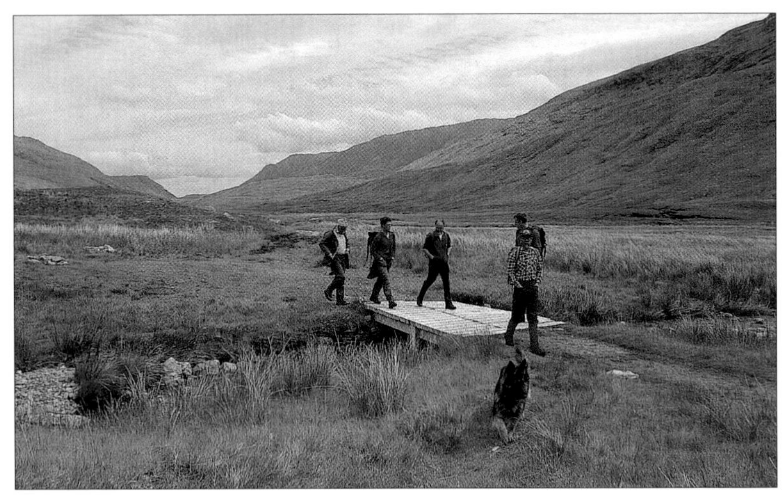

At the head of Glen Affric, heading to Gleann Lichd

SCALE 1:27 777 or about $2\frac{1}{4}$ INCHES to 1 MILE *3.6CM to 1KM*

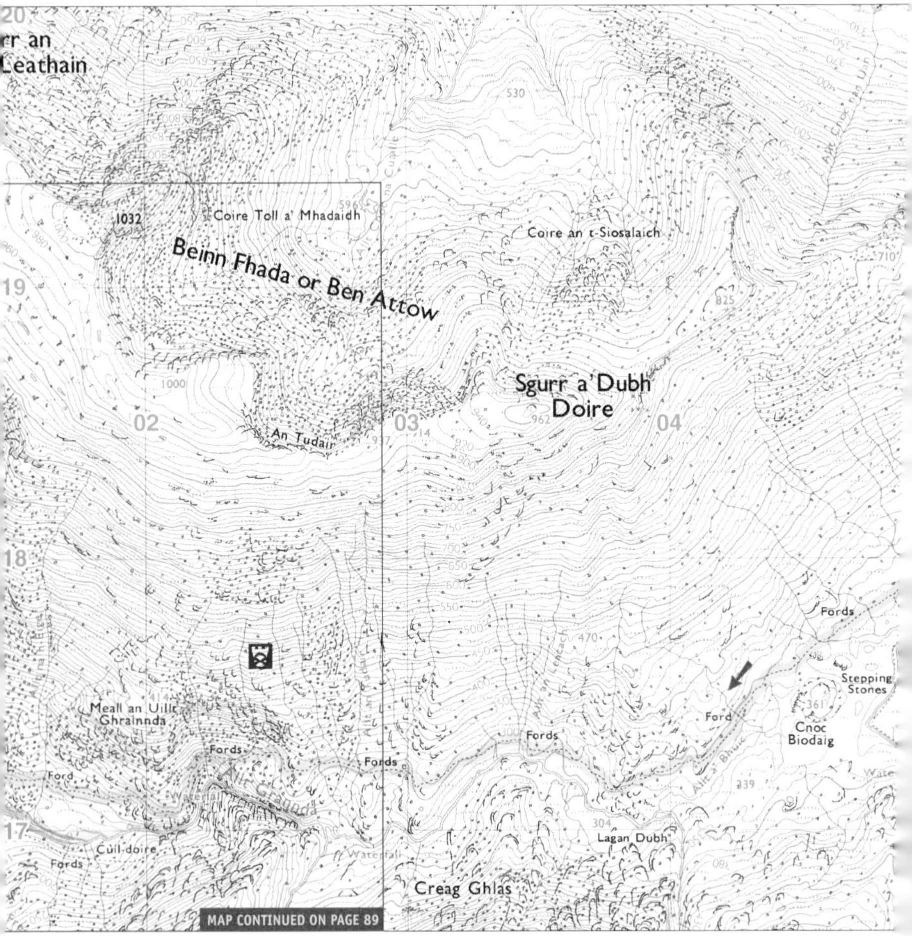

Beinn Fhada or Ben Attow
Coire Toll a' Mhadaidh
1032
Coire an t-Siosalaich
Sgurr a' Dubh Doire
962
825
An Tudair
02
03
04
19
18
17
Meall an Uillt Ghrainnda
Fords
Ford
Fords
Cuil-doire
Waterfall
Creag Ghlas
Lagan Dubh
304
Cnoc Biodaig
361
Stepping Stones
Ford
Fords
470
530

MAP CONTINUED ON PAGE 89

high Munros, A'Chralaig and Mullach Fraoch-choire, great grass and scree summits to inspire (or daunt) anyone.

The path eventually crosses a broad, low pass Ⓐ east of Ciste Dubh, continuing then gently downwards through the Allt a'Chòmlain to a ford and bridge at the very edge of Glen Affric and near Alltbeithe Youth Hostel, surely the most remote of all Scottish hostels.

From near the hostel, head south-west on a good, if occasionally wet, track into Fionngleann, making for Camban bothy Ⓑ, a remote base sometimes used by National Trust for Scotland rangers, or by walkers tackling the Scottish (and British watershed) which is shortly bound for the steep slopes of Beinn Fhada (or Ben Attow).

From Camban the route presses on, rising steadily to cross the watershed at a large cairn, beyond which a gentle

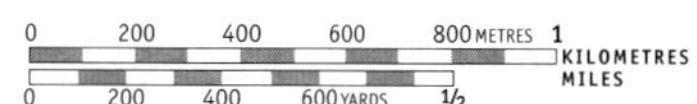

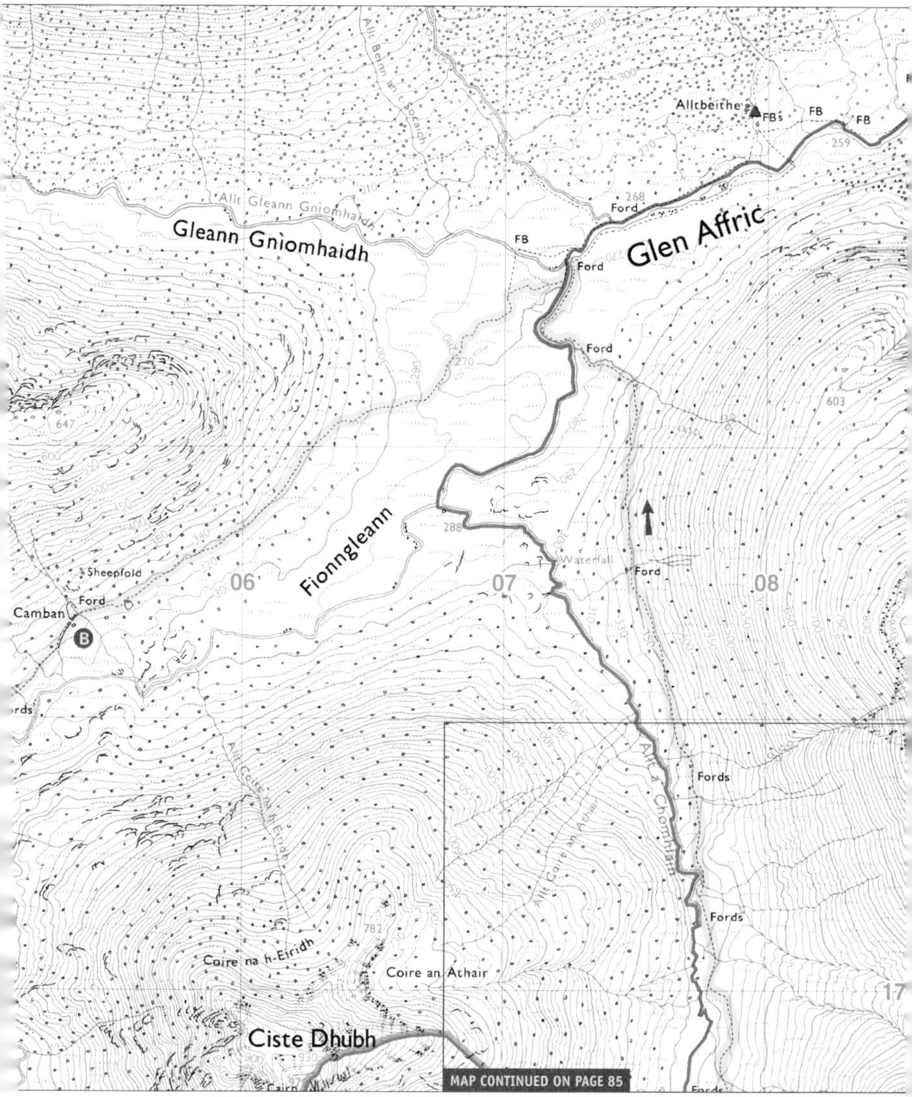

MAP CONTINUED ON PAGE 85

COUNTRYSIDE CENTRE
Lienassie
Sheepfold
Ford
Cattle Grid
Ruarach
Strath Croe
Croe Bridge
Abhainn Chonaig
Sheepfold
Innis a' Chrotha
Inchnacroe
Morvich
Mountain Rescue Post
Waterfall
Dam
OUTDOOR CENTRE
Ford
Sheep Pens
Ford
Beinn Bhuidhe
Allt Achadh Aire
Tobar an Tuirc (spring)
Sgurr na Moraich
Coire na Criche
Fàsach an t-Searraich
Sheepfold
Gleann Lic
River Croe
Coire na h-Uaighe
Beinn Bhuidhe
North East Face
Sgurr nan Saighead
Coire Druim na Staidhre
Bealach Buidhe
Drum Liath
Sìdhean Dubh
Kintail Fore
Coire a' Mhadaidh
North Face
Coire a' Mhuilt
Waterfall

plunge leads above the west-flowing waters of the Allt Grannda and its many tributaries into the long Gleann Lichd. The crossing also marks the passage from the ancient forest of Affric to that of Kintail.

Where the river doglegs south, it does so over a steep edge and provides a stunning waterfall. The path, though rough, is clear throughout, and leads into the head of Gleann Lichd, where Glenlichd House **C**, a former keeper's cottage, fits snugly into the embrace of the hills. From this remote habitation, now a university climbing hut, a splendid, motorable track leads all the way out through the glen (see Walk 22) to meet a surfaced lane not far from the Kintail Countryside Centre. ●

The waterfalls in Allt Grannda

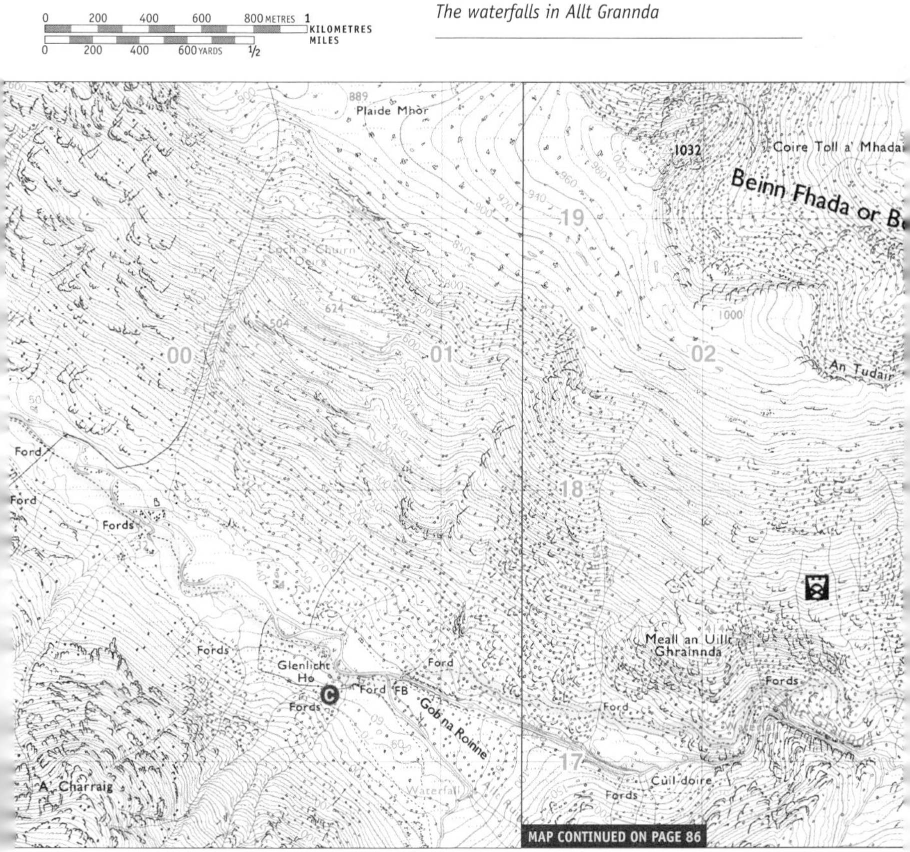

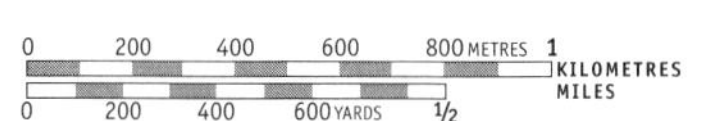

MAP CONTINUED ON PAGE 86

Further Information

The law and tradition as they affect walking in Scotland

Walkers following the routes given in this book should not run into problems, but it is as well to know something about the law as it affects access, and also something of the traditions which can be quite different in Scotland from elsewhere in Britain. Most of this is common sense, observing the country code and having consideration for others and their activities, which may be their livelihood.

It is often said that there is no law of trespass in Scotland. In fact there is, but the trespass itself is not usually a criminal offence. You can be asked to leave any property, and, technically, 'reasonable force' may be used to obtain your compliance – though the term is not defined. You can be charged with causing damage due to the trespass, but this would be hard to establish if you were just walking on open, wild, hilly country where, whatever the law, in practice there has been a long tradition of free access for recreational walking – something both the Scottish Landowners' Federation and the Mountaineering Council of Scotland do not want to see changed.

There are certain restrictions. Walkers should obey the country code and seasonal restrictions arising from lambing or stalking. Where there is any likelihood of such restrictions this is mentioned in the text and visitors are asked to comply. When camping, use a campsite. Camp fires should not be lit; they are a danger to moorland and forest, and really not necessary as lightweight and efficient stoves are now available.

Many of the walks in this book are on rights of way. The watchdog on rights of way in Scotland is the Scottish Rights of Way Society (SRWS), who maintain details on all established cases and will, if need be, contest attempted closures. They produce a booklet on the Scottish legal position (Rights of Way, A Guide to the Law in Scotland, 1991), and their green signposts are a familiar sight by many footpaths and tracks, indicating the lines of historic routes.

Crofting land, Port an-eorna

In Scotland rights of way are not marked on Ordnance Survey maps as is the case south of the border. It was not felt necessary to show these as such on the maps – a further reflection of the freedom to roam that is enjoyed in Scotland. So a path on a map is no indication of a right of way, and many paths and tracks of great use to walkers were built by estates as stalking paths or for private access. While you may traverse such paths, taking due care to avoid damage to property and the natural environment, you should obey restricted access notices and leave if asked to do so.

The only established rights of way are those where a court case has resulted in a legal judgment, but there are thousands of other 'claimed' rights of way. Local planning authorities have a duty to protect rights of way – no easy task with limited resources. Many attempts at closing claimed rights of way have been successfully contested in the courts by the Scottish Rights of Way Society and local authorities.

A dog on a lead or under control may also be taken on a right of way. There is little chance of meeting a free-range solitary bull on any of the walks. Any herds seen are not likely to be dairy cattle, but all cows can be inquisitive and may approach walkers, especially if they have a dog. Dogs running among stock may be shot on the spot; this is not draconian legislation but a desperate attempt to stop sheep and lambs being harmed, driven to panic or lost, sometimes with fatal results. Any practical points or restrictions will be given in the text of each walk. If there is no comment it can be assumed that the route carries no real restrictions.

Scotland in fact likes to keep everything as natural as possible, so, for instance, waymarking is kept to a minimum (the Scottish Rights of Way Society signposts and Forest Walk markers are in unobtrusive colours). In Scotland people are asked to 'walk softly in the wilderness, to take nothing except photographs, and leave nothing except footprints' – which is better than any law.

Scotland's hills and mountains: a concordat on access

This remarkable agreement was published early in 1996 and is likely to have considerable influence on walkers' rights in Scotland in the future. The signatories include organisations which have formerly been at odds - the Scottish Landowners' Federation and the Ramblers' Association, for example. However they joined with others to make the Access Forum (a full list of signatories is detailed below). The RSPB and the National Trust for Scotland did not sign the concordat initially but it is hoped that they will support its principles.

The signatories of the concordat are:

Association of Deer Management Groups
Convention of Scottish Local Authorities
Mountaineering Council of Scotland
National Farmers' Union of Scotland
Ramblers' Association Scotland
Scottish Countryside Activities Council
Scottish Landowners' Federation
Scottish Natural Heritage
Scottish Sports Association
Scottish Sports Council

They agreed that the basis of access to the hills for the purposes of informal recreation should be:

Freedom of access exercised with responsibility and subject to reasonable constraints for management and conservation purposes.

Acceptance by visitors of the needs of land management, and understanding of how this sustains the livelihood, culture and community interests of those who live and work in the hills.

Acceptance by land managers of the public's expectation of having access to the hills.

Acknowledgment of a common interest in the natural beauty and special qualities of Scotland's hills, and the need to work together for their protection and enhancement.

The forum point out that the success of the concordat will depend on all who manage or visit the hills acting on these four principles. In addition, the parties to the concordat will promote good practice in the form of:

- Courtesy and consideration at a personal level.
- A welcome to visitors.
- Making advice readily available on the ground or in advance.
- Better information about the uplands and hill land uses through environmental education.
- Respect by visitors for the welfare needs of livestock and wildlife.

Glossary of Gaelic Names

Most of the place-names in this region are Gaelic in origin, and this list gives some of the more common elements, which will allow readers to understand otherwise meaningless words and appreciate the relationship between place-names and landscape features. Place-names often have variant spellings, and the more common of these are given here.

aber mouth of loch, river
abhainn river
allt stream
auch, ach field
bal, bail, baile town, homestead
bàn white, fair, pale
bealach hill pass
beg, beag small
ben, beinn hill
bhuidhe yellow
blar plain
brae, braigh upper slope, steepening
breac speckled
cairn pile of stones, often marking a summit
cam crooked
càrn cairn, cairn-shaped hill
caol, kyle strait
ceann, ken, kin head
cil, kil church, cell
clach stone
clachan small village
cnoc hill, knoll, knock
coille, killie wood
corrie, coire, choire mountain hollow
craig, creag cliff, crag
crannog, crannag man-made island
dàl, dail field, flat
damh stag
dearg red
druim, drum long ridge
dubh, dhu black, dark
dùn hill fort
eas waterfall
eilean island
eilidh hind
eòin, eun bird
fionn white
fraoch heather
gabhar, ghabhar, gobhar goat
garbh rough
geal white
ghlas, glas grey
gleann, glen narrow, valley
gorm blue, green
inbhir, inver confluence
inch, inis, innis island, meadow by river
lag, laggan hollow
làrach old site
làirig pass
leac slab
liath grey
loch lake
lochan small loch
màm pass, rise
maol bald-shaped top
monadh upland, moor
mór, mor(e) big
odhar, odhair dun-coloured
rhu, rubha point
ruadh red, brown
sgòr, sgòrr, sgùrr pointed
sron nose
stob pointed
strath valley (broader than glen)
tarsuinn traverse, across
tom hillock (rounded)
tòrr hillock (more rugged)
tulloch, tulach knoll
uisge water, river

Rowan

map and compass – and know how to use them. Wear boots. Plan within your capabilities. If going alone ensure you leave details of your proposed route. Heed local advice, listen to weather forecasts, and do not hesitate to modify plans if conditions deteriorate.

Some of the walks in this book venture into remote country and others climb high summits, and these expeditions should only be undertaken in good summer conditions. In winter they could well need the skills and experience of mountaineering rather than walking. In midwinter the hours of daylight are of course much curtailed, but given crisp, clear late-winter days many of the shorter expeditions would be perfectly feasible, if the guidelines given are adhered to. THINK is the only actual rule. Your life may depend on that. Seek to learn more about the Highlands and your part in them, and continue to develop your skills and broaden your experience.

- Adherence to relevant codes and standards of good practice by visitors and land managers alike.
- Any local restrictions on access should be essential for the needs of management, should be fully explained, and be for the minimum period and area required.

Queries should be addressed to: Access Forum Secretariat, c/o Recreation and Access Branch, Scottish Natural Heritage, 2 Anderson Place, Edinburgh EH6 5NP.

Safety on the hills

The Highland hills and lower but remote areas call for care and respect. The idyllic landscape of the tourist brochures can change rapidly into a world of gales, rain and mist, potentially lethal for those ill-equipped or lacking navigational skills. The Scottish hills in winter can be arctic in severity, and even in summer, snow can lash the summits. It is essential that the walker is aware of these hazards, which are discussed more fully in the introduction.

At the very least carry adequate wind- and waterproof outer garments, food and drink to spare, a basic first-aid kit, whistle,

Mountain Rescue

In case of emergency the standard procedure is to dial 999 and ask for the police who will assess and deal with the situation.

First, however, render first aid as required and make sure the casualty is made warm and comfortable. The distress signal (six flashes/whistle-blasts, repeated at minute intervals) may bring help from other walkers in the area. Write down essential details: exact location (six-figure reference), time of accident, numbers involved, details of injuries, steps already taken; then despatch a messenger to phone the police.

If leaving the casualty alone, mark the site with an eye-catching object. Be patient; waiting for help can seem interminable.

Useful Organisations

Forest Enterprise
231 Corstorphine Road,
Edinburgh EH12 7AT.
Tel: 0131 334 0303; Fax: 0131 334 3047.

Regional Offices:
Scotland (North): 21 Church Street, Inverness IV1 1EL. Tel: 01463 232811; Fax: 01463 243846.
Scotland (South): 55/57 Moffat Road, Dumfries DG1 1NP.
Tel: 01387 272440; Fax: 01387 251491.

Historic Scotland
Longmore House, Salisbury Place,
Edinburgh EH9 1SH.
Tel: 0131 668 8800; website:
www.historic-scotland.gov.uk.

National Trust for Scotland
Wemyss House, 28 Charlotte Square,
Edinburgh EH2 4ET.
Tel: 0131 243 9300;
Fax: 0131 243 9301;
Email: information@nts.org.uk;
Website: www.nts.org.uk.

Ordnance Survey
Romsey Road, Maybush, Southampton
SO16 4GU.
Tel: 08456 050505;
Fax: (Public) 02380 792615;
Email: customerservices@ordsvy.gov.uk;
Website: www.ordnancesurvey.gov.uk.

Ramblers' Association
2nd Floor, Camelford House, 87-90 Albert Embankment, London SE1 7TW.
Tel: 020 7339 8585;
Fax: 020 7339 8501; Website:
www.ramblers.org.uk.

The old bridge, and hotel at Sligachan

Royal Society for the Protection of Birds (RSPB)
Abernethy Forest Reserve, Forest Lodge, Nethybridge, Inverness-shire PH25 3EF
Tel: 01479 821409

Scottish Natural Heritage
Battleby, Redgorton, Perth PH1 3EW.
Tel: 01738 627921; Fax: 01738 630583;
Contact: Media enquiries, Edinburgh (Tel: 0131 447 4784).

Scottish Wild Land Group
8 Hartington Place, Bruntsfield, Edinburgh EH10 4LE.
Tel: 0131 229 2094.

Scottish Youth Hostels Association
7 Glebe Crescent, Stirling FK8 2JA.
Tel: 01786 891400; Fax: 01786 891333;
Email: syha@syha.org.uk;
Website: www.syha.org.uk.

Public Transport
Bus Traveline: 0870 608 2 608
National Rail Enquires: 08457 48 49 50 (www.thetrainline.com)

ScotRail Railways Ltd.
Caledonian Chambers
87 Union Street
Glasgow G1 3TA
Website: www.scotrail.co.uk
08457 484950

Tourist organisations

Visit Scotland
23 Ravelston Terrace
Edinburgh EH4 3TP
Tel: 0131 332 2433
Fax: 0131 315 2906
Email: info@visitscotland.com
Website: www.visitscotland.net

Highlands of Scotland Tourist Board,
Peffery House
Strathpeffer
Inverness IV14 9HA.
Tel: 01997 421160
Fax: 01997 421168
Email: admin@host.co.uk
Website: www.host.co.uk

Local Tourist Information Centres
Broadford: 01471 822713
Kyle of Lochalsh: 01599 534276
Portree: 01478 612137

Ordnance Survey Maps of Kyle of Lochalsh

This area is covered by Ordnance Survey 1:50 000 (1$\frac{1}{4}$ inches to 1 mile or 2cm to 1km) scale Landranger map sheets 24, 32 and 33. These all-purpose maps are packed with information to help you explore the area. Viewpoints, picnic sites, places of interest and caravan and camping sites are shown, as well as public rights-of-way information such as footpaths and bridleways.

To examine the area in more detail and especially if you are planning walks, Ordnance Survey Explorer maps at 1:25 000 (2$\frac{1}{2}$ inches to 1 mile or 4cm to 1km) scale are ideal:

- 411 (Skye – Cullin Hills)
- 412 (Skye – Sleat)
- 413 (Knoydart, Loch Hourn & Loch Duich)
- 414 (Glen Shiel and Kintail Forest)
- 428 (Kyle of Lochalsh, Plockton & Applecross)

To get to Kyle of Lochalsh, use the Ordnance Survey Great Britain Route Travel Map at 1:625 000 (1 inch to 10 miles or 4cm to 25km) scale or Ordnance Survey Road Travel Map 1 (Northern Scotland, Orkney and Shetland) or 2 (Western Scotland and the Western Isles) at 1:250 000 scale (1 inch to 4 miles or 1 cm to 2.5km)

Ordnance Survey maps and guides are available from most booksellers, stationers and newsagents.